Simple Secrets

Couples Should Know

Bob & Emilie Barnes

HARVEST HOUSE PUBLISHERS

EUGENE, OREGON

Cover by Dugan Design Group, Bloomington, Minnesota

Cover photo © Stockbyte / Photolibrary

Every effort has been made to give proper credit for all stories, poems, and quotations. If for any reason proper credit has not been given, please notify the author or publisher and proper notation will be given on future printings.

SIMPLE SECRETS COUPLES SHOULD KNOW
Revised and updated version of *Growing a Great Marriage*
Copyright © 2008 by Bob and Emilie Barnes
Published by Harvest House Publishers
Eugene, Oregon 97402
www.harvesthousepublishers.com

Library of Congress Cataloging-in-Publication Data
Barnes, Bob, 1933-
    Simple secrets couples should know / Bob and Emilie Barnes. — [Rev. and updated ed.].
        p. cm.
    Rev. ed. of: Growing a great marriage. c1988.
    ISBN 978-0-7369-2254-8 (pbk.)
    1. Marriage—Religious aspects—Christianity. 2. Barnes, Emilie. I. Barnes, Emilie.
II. Barnes, Bob, 1933- Growing a great marriage. III. Title.
    BV835.B344 2008
    248.4—dc22

                                                                            2008027522

Printed in the United States of America

08 09 10 11 12 13 14 15 16 / VP-SK / 11 10 9 8 7 6 5 4 3 2 1

We dedicate this book to our two children, Jenny and Brad. You were a joy as children and continue to be a blessing as adults. Your cooperation has been greatly appreciated.

This book was possible only because some wonderful Christians took the time to contribute to our lives. Throughout the years there have been pastors, teachers, friends, and neighbors, seminars, retreats, tapes, and books—all have helped us formulate our marriage lifestyle. We give all the credit for our marriage to this tremendous Christian support.

The number one influence in our marriage has been the Bible. Without reading, studying, and applying its principles for life and marriage, Emilie and I could've ended up being another tragic statistic of marriage failure.

We want to encourage each of you to dedicate your life to showing the world through your marriage what Christ and the Church are all about. Our theme verse for growing a great marriage has been Ephesians 5:21: "Submit to one another out of reverence for Christ" (NIV). Only when we first humble ourselves before the Lord are we able to submit ourselves to one another. Keep pride off the throne of your life and let Jesus Christ be your power source.

Dedicate yourself to your mate. May Jesus Christ always be glorified in your marriage.

Contents

Why We're Sharing Secrets 7

1. I Pledge You My Troth 9
2. Looking for Love 13
3. What Is This Thing Called Love? 19
4. The Growing of a Wife-to-Be 27
5. The Growing of a Husband-to-Be 39
6. After the Wedding 51
7. Simple Secrets Every Wife Should Know 65
8. Simple Secrets Every Husband Should Know 83
9. The Oneness of Marriage 97
10. Making a Great Marriage 103
11. Growing Together Despite Differences 113
12. Meeting Your Wife's Needs 127
13. Meeting Your Husband's Needs 137
14. Four Marriage Health Builders 153
15. Keep Listening and Talking 157
16. Men Are Weird 171
17. Women Are Strange 177
18. Making Your Wife Your Best Friend 183
19. Money Matters in a Great Marriage 189
20. Secrets to Great Parenting 209
21. Shaping Great Children Through Discipline 225
22. The Law of Pursuit 239

Notes 247

Why We're Sharing Secrets

Simple Secrets Couples Should Know is born of a love story about two ordinary young people who fell in love, were married, and have enjoyed more than 52 years together. It's about how we grew a great marriage and how you can grow a great marriage too. Our book is not a manual full of foolproof theories, magic steps, or super formulas. Rather, we approach our view of marriage with a lifestyle flavor. Emilie and I want to share with you how we learned to be faithful to God's Word in our marriage and how He has been faithful to bless our life together. Ours is not the story of two perfect people, but two growing people who decided to be obedient to God's Word and to employ His principles to create a great marriage. Our story centers on the Lord Jesus Christ, the Son of God and the anchor of our life together. Without Him there would be no great marriage for us and no secrets to pass along.

We use the word *great* to describe our marriage in all humility. Only by being obedient to God and His Word can we call our marriage great. According to Romans 8:16-17, Emilie and I are God's children and joint heirs with Christ. In spite of all our differences, Emilie and I have a great marriage because we are both related to Christ and submitted to Him in each other. Wherever we travel we meet couples who are enjoying strong marriages. In each case we find two people who are willing to submit to God, submit to each other, and obey God's Word.

We have written from the foundation of Scripture and from the perspective of our life experience. As you will notice, Emilie wrote several of the chapters, and I wrote several. But every chapter reflects our combined thoughts on each subject. We have included practical examples from our marriage and the lives of many others we know. Furthermore, the content of this book has been influenced by our many years of reading, listening, and talking, and by countless stories, illustrations, and quotes on marriage we have collected. We have attempted to give proper credit to our sources. In some cases we don't remember the original source, but we felt the material was valuable to illustrate a point.

Our hearts ache from seeing the hurt and agony in marriages resulting from selfish mates who want their own way and who are unwilling to submit to one another. Marriage relationships are floundering, wracked by doubt, distrust, and infidelity. There is a general disregard for marriage vows. Our society has a false impression of what true marriage is because of the distorted view presented on television, in the movies, and even by other couples. Couples keep *receiving* the wrong message about marriage because our society keeps *sending* the wrong message about marriage.

Christian couples must learn how to build strong marriages. They need to work through the problems that spring up in various seasons of their relationship. Couples need to cultivate patience, good communication, trust, and commitment. They need to act on their marriage vows and adopt the spiritual dimension to see their marriages through to their golden years.

We trust that the secrets that have worked for us will become knowledge and insight that help you build the relationship you desire. We want our marriage to serve as a positive model that encourages and equips you to nurture a great and lasting marriage.

Bob & Emilie

I Pledge You My Troth

It is required in stewards that one be found faithful.

1 CORINTHIANS 4:2 NKJV

In the old wedding ceremonies, there was a phrase that read, "I pledge thee my troth." I often wondered, "What is a troth? Something to drink out of?" By looking the word up, I discovered that it originally meant a pledge to be true, faithful, loyal, and honest. It can also mean trust, reliability, and integrity in marriage. It's what we would call *fidelity* today. *Fidelity* is the word we use when we want to say that we will be faithful in marriage.

We exhibit fidelity, our troth, when we pour our energy into making our marriage function as God envisions it. Daily we're to live out what we promised to God at the altar.

> As rowers in a boat turn their backs to the shore and trust to the man at the helm, whose eye is fixed upon it; so should we proceed in duty through life—turn our backs from our anxious cares for the future, and leave the guidance of them all to God, who guides the helm.[1]

We also demonstrate our fidelity by building a fence around our marriage to protect our relationship from the enemy who would love to come in and destroy what God has put together. At times that protective fence might shut out trips, TV, music, work, sports, hobbies, and on occasion, even our children or church activities. We are not to let anything drain us of the energy we need to fulfill our part in a healthy marriage.

The maintenance of a happy marriage is critical to the security and happiness of our children. Stable families are more likely to produce well-adjusted children. A mother's commitment to the father of her children is one of the best investments she can make for the future of her children.

> *Say "no" to good things and save your "yeses" for the best.*

Fidelity is a calling to be faithful in every area of marriage. One of the chief drains on maternal energy is our participation in otherwise fine activities that end up robbing us of time and availability we need to succeed as wives and mothers.

Husbands have to strive to stay true to their commitments of their troths. We can become so consumed by our jobs, careers, and hobbies that all of our free time is taken up by pursuing these false gods. Look at a man's calendar and checkbook notations to determine his priorities. Both kinds of entries reveal what he really values. We are the spiritual leaders of our little flocks called families. We might not be able to change the whole world, but we have a powerful influence on our families.

One of my favorite mentors from the Bible is Joshua. He was such a man of conviction. He wasn't afraid to proclaim his faith in God. And one of my favorite passages in Scripture is found in Joshua 24:14-15. It says:

> Fear the LORD and serve Him in sincerity and truth; and put away the gods which your fathers served beyond the River and in Egypt, and serve the LORD. If it is disagreeable in your sight to serve the LORD, choose for yourselves today whom

you will serve: whether the gods which your fathers served which were beyond the River, or the gods of the Amorites in whose land you are living; but as for me and my house, we will serve the LORD.

We have the same decision to make today. We may have different gods to serve than the people of Joshua's day—our gods come in the form of careers, material possessions, food, vacations. Basically anything that causes us to take our eyes off the real God—our Lord—is a false god. When we took the pledge on our wedding day, we vowed that we would be true, faithful, loyal, and honest not only to one another but to the God we serve.

Are there activities in your life—a job, a club, a volunteer position, a church duty—that are taking you away from your main responsibility as a husband or wife? If so, you must reevaluate those time robbers and eliminate or scale back as necessary. Be brave like Joshua and stand and proclaim, "For me and my house, we will serve the LORD."

Secrets to Romancing Your Marriage

- ≶ Do a devotion and pray together.
- ≶ Go on a picnic this week.
- ≶ Support your mate when a relative discredits him or her.
- ≶ Do something special for each other's parents.
- ≶ Say "excuse me" and "forgive me" when you should.
- ≶ Don't overcommit your calendar. Save some time for your spouse.
- ≶ Don't answer a question for your spouse when the question is directed to your spouse.

2

Looking for Love

There is no fear in love; but perfect love casts out fear.

1 JOHN 4:18

So many people look for love in all the wrong places. Unfortunately the worldview of love is a distortion of real love; it focuses on fleeting passion and is often inspired by looks, material possessions, or successes rather than strong character. Any of us can get caught up in the world's version of love, so it's important to be reminded what it is all about. Helen Keller wrote this delightful explanation of love:

> I remember the morning that I first asked the meaning of the word "love." Miss Sullivan put her arm gently around me and spelled into my hand, "I love Helen."
>
> "What is love?" I asked.
>
> She drew me closer to her and said, "It is here," pointing to my heart.
>
> Her words puzzled me very much because I did not then understand anything unless I touched it. I smelled the violets in her hand and asked, half in words, half in signs, a question which meant, "Is love the sweetness of flowers?"
>
> "No," said my teacher.
>
> Again I thought. The warm sun was shining on us.
>
> "Is this not love?" I asked, pointing in the direction from which the heat came.

A day or two afterward…the sun had been under a cloud all day, and there had been brief showers, but suddenly the sun broke forth in all its southern splendor. Again I asked my teacher, "Is this not love?"

"Love is something like the clouds that were in the sky before the sun came out," she replied. Then in simpler words than these, which at that time I could not have understood, she explained: "You cannot touch the clouds, you know, but you feel the rain and know how glad the flowers and the thirsty earth are to have it after a hot day. You cannot touch love either; but you feel the sweetness that it pours into everything. Without love you would not be happy or want to play."

The beautiful truth burst upon my mind—I felt that these were invisible lines stretched between my spirit and the spirit of others.[1]

Recognizing the Foundation for Love

Before you can fully love your spouse, you must first realize from a biblical point of view why you are to love and how you are able to love. Christian growth isn't possible without obedience to the Scriptures.

The "natural man" must have a change of heart before he can make changes toward godly, outward obedience. Before love is given to another person, it must first be given to God. John 14:15 tells us Jesus said, "If you love Me, you will keep My commandments." When He was asked, "Which is the great commandment in the Law?" Jesus answered, "Love the Lord your God with all your heart and with all your soul and with all your mind." Then He said, "And the second is like it: 'Love your neighbor as yourself'" (Matthew 22:36-39 NIV).

Before we are able to truly love anyone else, God tells us that we are to love Him first. Men, you are to love God first, and then you can think about loving your wives. A godly woman yearns for a man who will worship God. She understands that if you can love God and put Him first in your life, you are then able to truly love her sacrificially.

A successful life is lived by one who has the right priorities in his life—being obedient to God's Word—and then putting into action what he knows to be true. Showing love is really just acting out—in all relationships—what you know to be true about the love of God.

If you have not made the decision to love and serve God in your life, then seek out a friend or pastor who can lead you through that process. Your understanding of love will increase dramatically!

Love is expressed when you stop living life your way and turn to living life God's way. When your marriage is based on God's principles, then you build a home that is secure and strong in the Lord.

> *But now faith, hope, love, abide these three; but the greatest of these is love.*
>
> 1 CORINTHIANS 13:13

Christian growth is a long, often difficult process. However, if husbands will be committed to the headship of Jesus in their families and to the authority of Scripture (2 Timothy 3:16), these priorities will give them the inspiration and courage they need to live responsibly. When husbands live like this, their wives and children will have a true sense of being loved.

All of us spend a good part of our lives earnestly searching for the most rewarding feeling of all—love. So what is this sought-after feeling? According to Scripture, it's much more than a fleeting emotion. Instead, *love is a decision* that we consciously make each day, and its presence is revealed in how we treat our spouses and others. When we love them, we choose to do what's best for them. The ultimate example of this kind of love is found in the primary love God has for us: "For God so loved the world, that He gave His only begotten Son, that whoever believes in Him shall not perish, but have eternal life" (John 3:16).

Now that's love! In spite of our not always choosing to do things His way, God gave us His only Son so that we might be forgiven and delight in His everlasting care. When we are able to capture even a glimpse of the magnitude of God's love, we gain an immense understanding of love's depth and power, and we discover that He has placed in us a capacity to love others far beyond our own ability. Our hearts become eager to love God, love ourselves, and love others. In fact, this becomes our main mission of life. This kind of love—*agape* love, the highest expression of love—can conquer all. It comes directly from heaven. When it enters our hearts, we are truly blessed with its rewards.

One of the roles a husband plays in the marriage is to be the protector of his wife's heart. Much of what we say and do will affect how she feels about our relationship. We know that love is much more than our feelings. However, since women tend to seek more sensitive, emotional connections, they will need more "I love you" statements and actions. I've learned that my wife needs to continually be reassured that I love her—morning, noon, and night. You think that once a day is sufficient—wrong! But the good news is that there are many ways in which to express love:

- a hug
- a kiss
- a note
- an e-mail
- a card
- a telephone call
- a gift
- a minivacation

Again, this message is for the men. Just because you told your wife at the altar that you loved her, it doesn't mean you're done telling her. There's an old southern saying that's so true: If Momma ain't happy, no one is happy! I know from experience that when Emilie feels confident in our love relationship, the meals are better, the children are more under control, there's more sex in our relationship, and the prettier her face shines. When our wives feel loved, it's a win-win situation.

Secrets to Romancing Your Wife

≫ Give your wife the night off. Fix dinner and do the dishes. Involve your children.

≫ Write a love letter to your wife. Tell her what you like about her and why she is so beautiful to you.

≫ Call her on the phone (when she is away from home), leave her a racy message, and tell her how you miss her and can't wait to see her tonight.

≫ It is better to stress *what* is right instead of *who* is right.

≫ Be willing to celebrate your wife's victories.

≫ Be aware of your wife's secret dream.

3

What Is This Thing Called Love?

*I feel that God would sooner we
did wrong in loving than never
love for fear we should do wrong.*
–Father Andrew

The word *love* is used so loosely today. We love our pets, but that's different than loving our mates. We can love a piece of music, our child, or the cool breeze of a spring morning. There's even the term "love" in tennis. We are capable of loving a close friend, our jobs, and our favorite meals. Falling in love is surely different than these other loves.

Learning more about this word *love* will help us understand how it can start out like any other emotion but then progresses to the point where both people desire a lifetime commitment together. Most of us know from past experiences that feeling "in love" can be misleading. Individuals who make decisions solely based on their feelings are usually unstable in other areas of their lives. But when love is based on more than feelings, it can be a stable foundation.

Scripture gives a very clear definition of what biblical love is about. First Corinthians 13:4-7 is probably the most-used Scripture at wedding ceremonies (in both religious and nonreligious weddings):

"Love is patient, love is kind. It does not envy, it does not boast, it is not proud. It is not rude, it is not self-seeking, it is not easily angered, it keeps no record of wrongs. Love does not delight in evil but rejoices with the truth. It always protects, always trusts, always hopes, always perseveres" (NIV).

Three Kinds of Love

Scripture describes three types of love. *Eros,* or erotic love, is driven by our physical attraction to another individual. We feel sexual desire toward that person. This type of love can arrive quickly and has a very strong appeal. Young love is usually this type. Men (because they are more visual than women) need to distinguish this as a "red flag" in a relationship. Eros certainly has its place in a marriage relationship. But eros love, if not discriminately used, can end up controlling your life. This form of love needs to be controlled *by* you. Don't be carried away by your senses during your early courtship. Eros love is also important to females, but it usually develops at a slower pace than with males. Men...be patient.

The second type of love mentioned in Scripture is *philo,* and it's often referred to as "brotherly love." This kind of love is one you share with a close friend. It comes about after spending a great deal of time with someone. That's why many marriage counselors recommend that courtship before marriage should last a minimum of one year. The more we know about an individual, the more likely we will become a "philo friend." Married love is healthiest when it grows out

> *Love is a fruit in season at all times, and within reach of every hand. Anyone may gather it, and no limit is set. Every-one can reach this love through meditation, spirit of prayer, and sacrifice, by an intense inner life.*
>
> –MOTHER TERESA

of a friendship. That's one of the purposes of dating. We get a chance to truly know the one we are going out with. This love is extremely important in finding your life mate. Philo love can be extended to your next door neighbor, a teammate in sports, a fellow worker, someone leading a small group of which you are a member.

Unlike eros, which is based on physical attraction, philo is developed as a person's character traits and interests become known by you, and you realize that those traits are ones you value. Your mate should be your favorite friend of the opposite sex. However, you can and should have other philo friends of your gender. Men tend to be loners. I encourage guys to have several other friends. If you are a married man, be careful with ladies who want to be friends. Married women need to take the same precaution with men who want friendship. We all need to have acquaintances, but we also must guard our hearts when it comes to having friends of the opposite sex.

Give your mate a big hug and tell them thank you for all they do to make your house a home.

We develop philo love when we spend time together—by going on picnics, hiking, sharing sports activities, going to the theater, watching movies, sharing a bag of popcorn. Our philo friends bring out the best in us. We love to be around them. They help civilize and inspire us.

Men and women are different in how they progress from the first meeting to sexual fulfillment. Males tend to go from eros love to philo love, but females often develop philo first and then go to eros love. Your wife or girlfriend might make a statement such as, "He grew on me!" What she is saying is that she developed eros love *after* getting to know you as a friend. Even after marriage never forget this need of the woman in your life. She wants you to be her number one friend of the opposite sex.

Philo love can be turned off by the words we use. Words that come from a place of anger, arrogance, self-pity, selfishness, resentment, and mistrust are negatives in your relationship. Guard your philo love with words that encourage, inspire, compliment, and show respect and appreciation.

Agape is the most common word for love in the New Testament. This love actively seeks to do the right thing for and meets the needs

Prayer of Saint Francis

Lord, make me an instrument of Thy peace;

where there is hatred, let me sow love;

where there is injury, pardon;

where there is despair, hope;

where there is darkness, light;

where there is sadness, joy.

O Divine Master,

grant that I may not so much

seek to be consoled as to console;

to be understood as to understand;

to be loved as to love;

for it is in giving that we receive;

it is in pardoning that we are pardoned;

and it is in dying that we are born to eternal life.

of the loved person. In this case, your spouse. Agape sacrifices personal feelings and needs to meet the needs of the other person. In agape we willingly give up our rights, our desires, and our demands to fulfill our partners' rights, desires, and demands. We may come home from work too tired to be kind or romantic to our spouses who need our loving attention. But agape love moves beyond what we feel like doing; it patiently seeks to discover and meet the needs of the other, no matter what the personal cost may be. So we rise above ourselves and meet the needs of our spouses.

All facets of love must reside within the realm of agape love. Our goal as Christians is to allow agape love to penetrate and rule the other two dimensions of love in our lives. In order to do this, we must first know Jesus Christ as our personal Savior and be submissive to His leadership. If you haven't made this basic commitment, you cannot move beyond eros and philo love. Many marriages can survive on these two dimensions of love alone, but it is God's will for Christians to allow agape love to dominate all of their relationships, bringing more depth and love to marriage. Agape love is the foundation of a relationship committed for life.

You can also have agape love for people to whom you are not married. Your children, your parents, your fellow Christians can all experience an agape love with you.

All three types of love should be experienced with that one person you wish to marry or are married to. The more secrets you know about love, the better you're able to love your mate.

Three Dimensions of Biblical Love

AGAPE
Doing what is right
even if it involves
negative feelings

PHILO
Responding to someone's
needs affectionately and
with positive emotions,
but always within
the guidelines of
agape love.

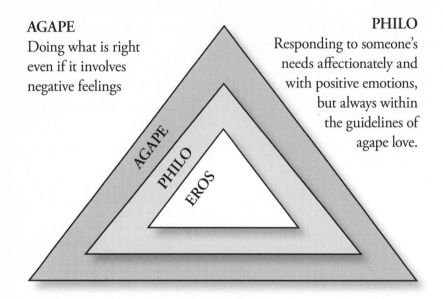

EROS
Becoming emotionally,
physically, and
sexually involved with
another person, but
always within the
guidelines of agape
and philo love

Secrets to Romancing Your Marriage

≫ Share a bubble bath together.

≫ Write a love note to your spouse with lipstick on your bathroom mirror.

≫ Buy your wife her favorite stuffed animal.

≫ Decide on the spur-of-the-moment to take a day off and do something together.

≫ Compliment your spouse today.

≫ Send your husband a letter sealed with a kiss (use your brightest lipstick).

≫ Turn to your mate in public and whisper, "I'm glad I married you!"

≫ Plan a second honeymoon.

4

The Growing of a Wife-to-Be

We know that in all things God works
for good with those who love him, those
whom he has called according to his purpose.

ROMANS 8:28 TEV

Irene, a Jewish girl born in Brooklyn, New York, is the oldest of five children. Her mother died during the birth of Irene's baby sister. And Papa, a gifted tailor, died a few years later, leaving teenaged Irene to raise her brothers and sisters. Jobs and money were in California, so the young family headed for Hollywood to make a life for themselves.

As a young adult, Irene designed and sewed tennis dresses for movie stars in the early 1920s. She worked hard to support herself and her brothers and sisters. At 29 she met Otto Klein, a 40-year-old chef for Paramount Studios. Irene married Otto in 1930.

Irene badly wanted children, but Otto wouldn't hear of it. As a German Jew and a veteran of World War I, Otto had barely escaped the war with his life. He wasn't about to bring children into such an angry world. Twice Irene became pregnant and twice he forced her to have an abortion. When she became pregnant a third time, Irene refused to terminate the pregnancy. In July 1934, a beautiful son, Edmund Francis Klein, was born to Otto and Irene. Four years later, on April 12, 1938, Emilie Marie Klein was born. Otto adored his baby daughter, but his young son became the abused victim of a father filled with hatred from the abuse he suffered as a child.

Otto was a creative and artistic man. As an orphan in Vienna, Austria, he was placed in the palace to be a kitchen helper. His exceptional ability gained him training by the finest chefs in Europe, and Otto became an expert Viennese chef. He escaped war-torn Europe, traveling first to New York and then to Hollywood. There he became a chef to movie stars—Clark Gable, Mickey Rooney, Lana Turner, Greta Garbo, Mario Lanza, Douglas Fairbanks, Judy Garland, and many more. Yet deep inside this successful man was a little boy still hurting from the loss of his parents.

Otto turned to alcohol to escape his pain, jeopardizing his career and his family. Otto's drinking fueled his angry perfectionism, resulting in violent outbursts at the shortcomings of his coworkers, wife, and children.

Irene's fear for the safety of herself and her children smothered her fun-loving, sanguine temperament. Edmund stored his anger for his abusive father, releasing it later through rebellion. And Emilie—that's me—became a very bashful, quiet child.

I have only a few happy memories of my father. When I was nine years old, we moved to Long Beach, California, where Daddy managed a restaurant called Ormando's. He would take me on walks along the beach, and we would fish off the pier. He gave me a beautiful blue bicycle on my tenth birthday.

Daddy lost his job at Ormando's due to his temper and drinking problem. Edmund, who was almost 14 at the time, began his years of rebellion. Then Daddy became very ill. He refused to listen to his doctors. Instead he got mad at them and demanded that they make him well.

Because of my father, the emotional thermometer in our home was almost always on high. It was my job to try to keep peace—I was able to cool Daddy's temper at times. He adored me and never abused me. But I hurt inside because of what he did to my mother and brother. I suffered from nightmares, and I wished Daddy would die—relieving us of the control he held over us with his hot temper.

Daddy didn't let Mama cook very often because she didn't meet his gourmet standards. But she was also a great cook. Her corned beef cabbage rolls and other Jewish meals are a delicious memory. Occasionally Mama and Daddy would prepare a meal together, and I would sit on the drain board watching and learning. Those were happy days for me—probably because Daddy wasn't drinking on those days.

The summer after my eleventh birthday, Daddy died and we were released from his bondage. I cried as I looked toward heaven wondering about the afterlife. But I quickly pushed those thoughts out of my mind. Mama was now a single mother with two children to care for. Being unemployed and uninsured, Daddy left us with hospital and doctor bills.

It is far better to forgive and forget than to hate and remember.

My aunt and uncle kept us afloat financially and helped my mother open up a small dress shop in Long Beach. We lived in a three-room apartment behind the store—kitchen, living room, and one bedroom. It was perfect for our needs. We gave Edmund the bedroom, and Mama and I slept together in a Murphy bed (one that folds out of the wall) in the living room. Mama gave me the responsibility of caring for those three rooms while she ran the dress shop. I painted the whole apartment myself, even though I had never painted in my life. I decorated the walls and, with help from Mama, made curtains, tablecloths, and chair covers. I planted flowers in our window box and kept the bathroom and kitchen spotless. Under Mama's direction I prepared the meals and washed the laundry.

Mama was a Proverbs 31 woman and didn't even know it. She was a hard worker, often working at the shop late into the night. She watched for bargains to make our money go farther. Together we transformed our simple apartment into a haven of peace.

At age 16 I attended a modeling class at the Wilma Hastings Modeling School (my instructor later became Mrs. Frank Sinatra). It was there that I met Esther, the most talented, beautiful, and natural model in our class. Esther later went to New York and became a high fashion model, appearing on the cover of several fashion magazines.

Esther stayed with me a week that summer. We went to the beach, worked in our dress shop, and played "fashion show." One evening we went to the movies. There I met Bill Barnes. Bill wanted to date Esther, but Esther and I had made an agreement that we would only double date. Esther told Bill that he would have to find a date for her girlfriend Emilie. Bill's identical twin, Bob, owed him a favor, so Bob Barnes became my blind date.

I was immediately attracted to Bob. He had a deep tan and wore denim pants, a white T-shirt, and saddle shoes. He was a mature college student, athletic and strong. He opened the door for me, displayed gracious manners, and carried himself with an air of gentleness. There was something very different about him.

Esther and I had been experimenting with cigarettes and planned to smoke in front of these college men to show them how mature we were. When Esther offered me a cigarette, I heard a voice inside me say, "Don't do it!" So I refused, and was I ever glad. Later we discovered that Bill and Bob didn't smoke, and I wanted Bob to be impressed with me.

I was shy, bashful, and very quiet during our blind date. I figured that if I didn't talk a lot, I wouldn't say the wrong thing and reveal my age. I didn't want to blow it with Bob Barnes.

I was absolutely shocked when Bob called me for a real date. On

> *By wisdom a house is built, and by understanding it is established; and by knowledge the rooms are filled with all precious and pleasant riches.*
>
> PROVERBS 24:3-4

the day of our date, I cleaned the house, baked cookies, washed and set my hair, polished my nails, and washed and ironed clothes. I prepared the atmosphere by lighting candles and boiling cinnamon sticks on the stove to give the apartment a homey aroma. I wanted everything to be perfect—even the things he wouldn't see when he came to pick me up.

Being a focused, devoted homemaker, I won the heart of my man—except for one area. I was a Jewish girl, and Bob was a committed Christian. My aunts and uncles were outraged that Mama allowed me to date a Gentile—worse yet, a "dyed-in-the-wool Baptist" as they called him. "You are making a big mistake, Irene," they told Mama. "He'll never amount to anything. He's not good enough for our Emilie. They'll have a miserable life. She's too young so send him away. Better yet, send her away."

Even though I didn't know it at the time, God was in control. By the time I was 16, our relationship was growing deep and serious. Bob's family was praying for me during those dating months as Bob patiently read the Scriptures to me, took me to church, directed me to messages by Billy Graham, and introduced me to his Christian friends. One verse that pierced my heart was John 14:6: "Jesus answered, 'I am the way and the truth and the life. No one comes to the Father except through me'" (NIV). I asked myself, *Is Jesus the Messiah our people are waiting for?*

Then I read Romans 6:23, "The wages of sin is death, but the gift of God is eternal life in Christ Jesus our Lord" (NIV). *Eternal life—is that the answer to an 11-year-old's questions about life after death? Can I have life forever and ever by believing in Jesus Christ and receiving Him into my heart? Is dying merely a change of address from earth to heaven?*

Bob gently guided me into the family of God. One night, in the quietness of my room, I knelt, opened the door of my heart, and invited the Lord Jesus—Messiah Yeshua—into my life. I asked Him to change me and give me a heart ready to serve Him. I asked Him to take control of me and guide me on a path that would please Him.

Having cleared the only hurdle between us, I wanted to marry

Bob Barnes and build a healthy, happy, spiritual home free from abuse and anger—a home with harmony, love, and the fragrance of Jesus. I knew we could have that kind of home, even though the path would be rocky at times. Bob and I were committed to the common goal of serving the Lord and serving each other. We could survive with God's help.

For God so loved the world, that He gave His only Begotten Son, that whoever believes in Him should not perish, but have eternal life.

JOHN 3:16

The criticism from my family grew strong, especially after we announced our engagement. My aunt and uncle offered to send me to one of the best finishing schools in Europe, buy me a car and a wardrobe, and provide me an unlimited expense account if I would not marry Bob. But my heart now belonged to God and to Bob. I had already received the greatest gift—God's Son, Messiah Jesus—with no strings attached. I told my aunt and uncle that I loved them, but I was going to marry Bob and establish a Christian home.

In September 1955, Bob—age 22—and I—age 17—were married. Yes, my relatives' hearts were broken. Family pressure was heavy on Mama who agreed to sign for me to marry at my young age. But, thank God, I was not disowned or "buried" as some Jews are when they marry outside the faith. My family didn't think our marriage would last more than a few months. But we had a loving God guiding our hearts and lives.

Shortly after our wedding, I began my senior year of high school, and Bob began his first year of teaching. I wasn't much older than his students. Bob helped me with term papers, signed my report cards, and attended senior activities with me. I received the homemaker of the year award, starred in the senior play, and served as student body secretary as the only married student at Long Beach Poly High School.

After graduation I kept house, worked in the dress shop, and later took a job with a bank. I wanted a family, but Bob felt we should wait until we could afford a house and he was secure in his school district. Three years later our daughter Jennifer Christine was born.

Just a few months after Jennifer arrived, we became parents to three more children. My brother Edmund's wife left for the market one day and never returned home, walking out on her husband and three preschool children—Tawney, Keri, and Kevin. We have seen her only once in more than 40 years, and she has only recently contacted her children. Edmund became very depressed and was unable to care for his children. Bob and I felt the children needed love and stability, so we asked Edmund if he would let us take them into our home. We soon became legal guardians for Tawney, Keri, and Kevin.

Mothering four children under the age of four was an exhausting job. I cooked, baked, cleaned, washed, ironed, and did everything I could to create a loving home for our family. I made all the children's clothes, plus my own. Whenever Bob wasn't refereeing football or basketball games, he was home by 4:00 p.m., which was a great help to me. I was happy that my childhood responsibilities had equipped me with the tools I needed—another proof that God works all things together for His purposes.

A few weeks after Edmund's children came, I discovered that I was pregnant. I was so sick with number five that it was difficult to carry on with the other four. One day I was so sick that I took the four kids into the backyard, spread a blanket on the grass, and passed out. I didn't care if they ate dirt or snails while I slept; I wouldn't need to feed them lunch.

In May 1960 our son Bradley Joe Barnes was born, giving us five children under five years of age—and I was only 21. My mother was still running the dress shop and unable to help me. Bob was a great help, but he had a profession, night classes, and a part-time refereeing job. I survived the next few years until Edmund remarried. His wife had two children, so when Edmund's three went back to him, they had a family of seven.

By this time Mama's business had faltered, and she filed for bankruptcy. She lost what little she had and slipped into a deep depression. She was in her early sixties with no home, no job, and no future.

We invited Mama to live with us until she could reorganize her life. Mama's visit turned out to be another step in the path of God's plan. Being in our home, she attended church with us and the Spirit of God touched her heart. In 1964 Mama invited the Messiah into her life. She was the only one of my family members to come into the Christian family. But I'm not giving up on my family. John 14:14 says, "If you ask me for anything in my name, I will do it" (TEV). I'm trusting our Lord for each of my family members to come to know Jesus, and He will answer in His time.

> *Forgiveness saves the expense of anger, the cost of hatred, the waste of spirits.*
>
> —HANNAH MORE

Bob and I continued to raise our family. We were committed to God, family, love, goals, and raising responsible adults. I worked at being industrious, creative, and very organized in our family life, which gave me "more hours in my day"—the title of my first book and the basis for my future ministry.

At age 29 I became the first chairwoman of the Newport Beach Christian Women's Club. That year I was asked to speak to more than 800 women at a conference in Palm Springs. I was so naïve and absolutely scared to death. But the response to my testimony overwhelmed me. Other chairwomen asked me to speak at their meetings. A longtime Christian friend, who supported me in prayer that day, answered, "She'll come," and started booking dates. Since that time I have spoken to several hundred Christian Women's Clubs.

In 1971 we moved from Newport Beach to Riverside, California. I was 33 years old. Our years in Newport Beach had gained us some very close friends and church relationships. We had grown spiritually so much at Mariners Church that it was hard to begin again. By this time Mama had moved into a senior citizens' building. She attended Bible studies, met others her age, and grew through the great teaching she received.

People often asked us, "Why did you move from the beach to the desert?" In the beginning years, that was hard to answer, but as we look back over our married life, we can very clearly see why God had us make that move. If not for Riverside, we would never have met some people that were very beneficial to our lives. God knew better than we did that we needed to be there for all those years. One great verse of Scripture that gives us that assurance is Jeremiah 29:11: " 'For I know the plans that I have for you,' declares the LORD, 'plans for welfare and not for calamity to give you a future and a hope.' "

Our move to Riverside wasn't easy for me. I was homesick for our friends. It was during this time that I met Florence Littauer. We had much in common as speakers, and our husbands encouraged us to write a seminar for women. In the spring of 1973, Florence and I taught our first "Feminar" to only a handful of women. But it was a beginning. God was paving the way for our ministries. Florence founded C.L.A.S.S. (Christian Leaders and Speakers' Seminar), and Bob and I founded the "More Hours in My Day" seminars. We are just two ordinary women open to God's leading, with two supportive, encouraging husbands cheering us on.

For some people those years may have been wasted years in the desert, but God knew what He was doing in our lives. He was grooming us in His Word, letting us get to know people who would help us in future ministry, and having our daughter meet a young man who would give us three wonderful grandchildren. Yes, Romans 8:28 has certainly been true in our lives: "And we know that God causes all things to work together for good to those who love God, to those who are called according to *His* purpose."

In Sickness and in Health

In the summer of 1997, I felt run down, fatigued, and not at all like myself. I was losing weight and energy and found it very difficult to travel for my speaking ministry. At the urging of my daughter and my Bob, I reluctantly went to my doctor and had a blood test. Upon getting the results, he suggested that I see an oncologist. I'll never forget the day the doctor said I had cancer. The air was sucked out of my lungs. I received that news as a death sentence. Through a string of events, we journeyed to Newport Beach to meet with a leading oncologist for a second opinion. After tests and a very thorough examination, he declared that I had non-Hodgkins lymphoma with a large tumor the size of a football wrapped around my intestine. Immediately I began chemotherapy and radiation treatments for my tumor. This was the beginning of a three-year journey of trying to cure my cancer.

This diagnosis and the treatments required to treat the cancer eventually required us to relocate back to Newport Beach for treatment. Commuting from Riverside to our new doctor was not practical. We sold our home and moved. It was a sad day but also a wonderful homecoming as we reconnected with our old friends and our old church.

After three years of cancer treatment, the doctor could not keep me in remission. In May 2000, we flew to Seattle, Washington, to the Fred Hutchinson Cancer Center. There I was to receive a bone marrow transplant, donated by a healthy 23-year-old Canadian young man. We stayed there for five months, until we were able to be released, return home, and follow up with our oncologist in Newport Beach.

It was the longest and hardest five months in my life. I was challenged in my faith, by the medical profession, and by God's plan for my life. Yet, during this period, God gave me two great verses of Scripture that helped shape my faith and my life:

> This sickness is not unto death, but for the glory of
> God, that the Son of God may be glorified through it.

JOHN 11:4 NKJV

Weeping may last for the night, but a shout of
joy comes in the morning.

PSALM 30:5

As of this writing I am cancer-free and have been restored to good
health and am able to continue my writing and speaking schedule.
This summer I will be able to celebrate the marriage of my donor from
Toronto, Canada. Yes, God has taken a long round-about way to make
me into the person I am today. I would have chosen a different route,
but His ways are not always my ways. However, I'm well pleased with
the way He has made me.

We each have a different story in life. I trust that you can see the
hand of God working in you. I am the person I am today because of
all that God has orchestrated in me.

Secrets to Romancing Your Husband

- ⇝ Show respect and admiration toward your husband when
  in public.
- ⇝ Share your most secret ambitions with your spouse.
- ⇝ Discuss what you would most like to be remembered for.
- ⇝ What is one way that your husband can show you that he
  really loves you? Tell him.
- ⇝ Ask your husband how you can show him love.
- ⇝ Pack a special lunch for your husband. Include all his
  favorites and a special love note.

5

The Growing of a Husband-to-Be

It was planted in good soil beside abundant
waters, that it might yield branches and
bear fruit and become a splendid vine.

EZEKIEL 17:8

My twin brother, Bill, and I were born in the middle of the Depression on a dirt farm outside Abilene, Texas. My father, J.K. Barnes, was 21 and my mother, Gertie Bell Barnes, was 18. Dad was a sharecropper working for 75¢ a day with the opportunity to grow much of our food. We lived a long way out of town and down a long dirt road. We had plenty of mud in the winter and dust in the summer, making it almost impossible for Mom to keep the house clean. I vividly remember catching rainwater in buckets as it dripped through our leaky roof. Some nights we would wake up soaking wet in bed from a previously undetected leak.

Bill and I weighed a total of 15 pounds at birth—Mom weighed only 84 pounds. Due to the crowded womb, Bill and I were born clubfooted—both of Bill's feet and my right foot are affected. Being poor farmers, my parents were resigned to Bill and me growing up crippled. But my grandfather heard of a young doctor who performed corrective surgery on clubfooted children. So Dad and Mom, with no money, took us to the Crippled Children's Hospital in Dallas, hoping Dr. Hodges would perform the needed surgery. God led my grandfather to assist with the finances, and Bill and I underwent two years of treatments through which God healed our deformities. I am very grateful to my generous grandfather and a knowledgeable doctor. Without their help, my physical development and athletic achievements would have been severely limited.

My grandfather was a very godly man who brought his family up attending the little white Methodist church next to the cemetery. I remember going to that church as a boy and singing grandfather's favorite hymn, "In the Garden." I still flash back to those wonderful Sunday services whenever I sing that hymn today.

In 1939 my parents moved off the farm to improve our standard of living. Dad took an eight-to-five job with the El Paso Natural Gas Company in Jal, New Mexico, a very small town in the southeast corner of the state. In Jal I entered the first grade. My teacher, Mrs. Hulse, was a sweet, warm, and friendly lady who made a big impression on me.

We lived in Jal for three years. I remember coming home from church one Sunday morning and hearing the radio bulletin announcing that the Japanese had bombed Pearl Harbor. Later that evening President Franklin D. Roosevelt explained the details of the attack. Most of us had never heard of Pearl Harbor, but we soon learned much about it and have never forgotten it.

The attack on Pearl Harbor played a large role in our family moving from New Mexico to Southern California. My dad's brother George worked in the oil fields in Long Beach, California. George promised Dad a good-paying job, so with little money in his pocket, Dad hitchhiked to California. After two very long months, Mom and her three sons (by this time my younger brother Kenneth Eugene had been born) boarded a train for Los Angeles. At that time the trains were full of military personnel traveling from one base to another. Mom had the good fortune to meet the famous movie star Lew Ayres aboard our train, returning to Hollywood from army boot camp. He took an interest in our family and served as our personal escort for the rest of the journey to our new state and new lifestyle.

In those days Hollywood was the home of the stars, and we were so excited to live in the same area as Clark Gable, Lew Ayres, Gene Autry, Roy Rogers, Janet Leigh, Humphrey Bogart, Ava Gardner, Betty Grable, and many others.

Living quarters in Long Beach were hard to find during the early war years. In addition to the increased military population, Long Beach was the home of thousands who worked in plants building planes and ships. But God was watching over our family; Dad was able to find a three-bedroom home nestled in the oil fields of Long Beach. Our rent was high at $45 a month, but we were glad to have a place to live.

Long Beach was the community that shaped my identity as a young man. I obtained my education there, from elementary school through a master's degree in education from California State University at Long Beach. During my school years, I was very involved in athletics, music, paper routes, student government, and church activities. I have many fond memories of those years.

> *Our greatest weakness lies in giving up. The most certain way to succeed is always to try one more time.*
>
> –Thomas Edison

When we moved to California, Mom and Dad joined Bethany Baptist Church. I vividly remember Easter Sunday in 1945 when, as a 12-year-old, I responded to the preaching of the gospel and accepted Jesus Christ as my personal Savior. I will never forget the excitement I felt after making the most important decision of my life. That night I was baptized and began my new life in Christ. Because I had been raised in the church by two very warm and loving parents, my conversion was a natural step in my growth.

As a teenager I was glad to be a Christian because I saw the Lord do so much for my relatives, neighbors, and friends. It seems like I always had good Christian models to influence me. Art Clausen, who taught a teen Bible study at church on Thursday nights, made a significant impact on my life. Our pastor at that time, Pastor Warren Glover, lifted weights at the YMCA. I was impressed that my pastor was athletic.

During my high school years, our church was very active in softball and basketball leagues. Our coach, Lloyd Arthur, played a large role in the good direction of my life. We had some outstanding teams that won many Southern California championships in both sports. The sports program was a great outreach ministry for our church. We saw many young men come to know the Lord by attending church to play on our teams.

From the Easter Sunday of my conversion to September 30, 1955, when I married Emilie, my church played an extremely important role in my life. While attending this little church, I determined the kind of man, husband, and father I wanted to become. I'm so thankful for the many fine pastors we had. Each one made a special impression on my life. Even though I can't remember any specific sermons, I clearly remember that my pastors taught from the Bible. I began to rely on God's Word, and I determined to learn it very well.

As a teenager I realized that I wanted a godly woman for a wife, one who loved the Lord as I did and who wanted to raise a family by Christian principles. I dated many girls, both Christians and non-Christians. I was looking for a girl whose heart beat to serve the Lord and who held solid values and goals. Up to the summer before my senior year in college, I had not found the one special girl I had been praying for. I figured that perhaps God would lead me to a special girl during sorority and fraternity rush week in the fall.

One night in August, my brother Bill called and told me he had met a very special girl named Esther who was staying with her friend Emilie. Bill wanted to date Esther, but she wouldn't go out with him unless he found a date for her hostess. After several of his buddies turned him down, Bill decided that I could help him out since I owed him a favor.

Little did I know that this blind date was going to change my life forever. I remember my first impression of Emilie Klein on that warm August evening. She was real cute! She had a beautiful tan and wore a full black skirt with a white off-the-shoulder blouse. We went out for a soda and conversation after the girls' modeling class. As we took the girls home to the apartment Emilie shared with her mother and brother, I knew Emilie Klein was special. I walked her to the door and asked for her phone number because I wanted to see her again. The next day I called, and we went out together that evening, the next evening, and several evenings after that. I was beginning to believe that Emilie Klein was the special girl God had prepared for me.

September came and I started my senior year in college. I took Emilie to a "welcome back" party hosted by one of my fraternity brothers. That evening I learned two very troubling facts that seemed to alter what I thought was God's direction for me. First, Emilie was only 16, far too young for me. Second, she was Jewish. At the end of the evening, I told her that I wouldn't be calling her for a while because I would be very busy with my new classes.

I really thought I would meet my very special *older* girl during rush week. But two weeks passed, and my special girl hadn't appeared. I wondered what God was doing. The first football game was coming up, and I didn't have a date. So I picked up the phone, called Emilie, and asked her to go to the football game with me. Her yes changed the course of both our lives. After that evening I knew she was God's special woman for me. I wasn't sure how He was going to solve the two problems of age and religion, but I knew He could do it somehow.

One surprising answer to prayer occurred when Emilie's mother permitted her to attend church with me and my family. It was a miracle because Emilie had recently completed Hebrew school and had been confirmed in her Jewish faith. Emilie had many questions about Christ and Christianity as she heard Pastor Claude Sailhammer preach the gospel. Her questions gave me opportunities to open my Bible and give her clear, scriptural answers.

On many Sunday nights after church, I parked my car in the alley behind Emilie's apartment while Emilie and I listened to Billy

Graham's *Hour of Decision* broadcast on the car radio. I'm very thankful for Billy Graham and his ministry. He was a messenger God used to share the gospel with Emilie. One Sunday night as we listened to the broadcast, we were surprised by the beam of a flashlight shining in the car window. I rolled down the window to hear the husky voice of a police officer asking, "What are you doing?" Somewhat startled, I told him we were listening to Billy Graham on the radio. "Oh, sure!" he replied disbelievingly. But after listening for a few moments, he went on his way.

One evening Emilie and I were sitting on the sofa in her living room. I held her face between my hands and looked into her eyes. I told her that I loved her very much, but I couldn't ask her to marry me. "Why not?" she asked, tears filling her eyes.

I quoted 2 Corinthians 6:14, which was engraved on my heart and mind: "Do not be yoked together with unbelievers" (NIV). Then I gave her three reasons why I could not marry her.

First, a Christian cannot marry a non-Christian because of what an unequal marriage will do to the non-Christian. There is no fellowship between light and darkness. The marriage will have a divided loyalty. I said, "If I promise to marry you, I am choosing to spend my life with someone who is going in a completely different direction. We will move farther apart. I have no right to draw you into a relationship that is doomed to disharmony."

Second, I couldn't marry an unbeliever because of what it might do to me. If I disobeyed God on this issue, I might compromise my standards later and disobey Him again and again. Too much was at stake if I disobeyed God's clear command about marriage.

Emilie asked, "But what if I become a Christian after we are married?" I told her that marriage is not a mission field. God never called Christians into an unequal marriage to convert the unbelieving partner.

Third, I said that an unequal marriage would not honor God. He did not create us and redeem us so we could live for ourselves. God placed us here to glorify Him. A Christian home is the only home that can glorify God. When a husband and wife both belong to Jesus Christ and live in obedience to Him, they provide a vital witness to the society around them.

Emilie was shocked. She had taken a very special interest in me as the type of man she could love and eventually marry. In her innocence she asked me, "How do I become a Christian?" And from that moment she began to ask herself if Jesus Christ was the Messiah her Jewish people were awaiting. After several months of seeking answers, she prayed one evening at bedtime, "Dear God, if You have a Son, and if Your Son is Jesus our Messiah, please reveal Him to me!" Emilie expected a voice to answer her immediately. But God did reveal Himself to her within a few weeks.

> *Drink water from your own well—share your love only with your wife. Let your wife be a fountain of blessing for you.*
>
> PROVERBS 5:15,18 NLT

One Sunday morning Emilie responded to Pastor Sailhammer's challenge to accept Jesus Christ as her personal Savior. That evening she was baptized. I was thrilled! God had answered one of my two prayerful questions. Emilie's mother didn't completely understand what had happened, but she admitted that if her daughter was happy, she was happy.

As I approached graduation and my student teaching assignments, I realized that I would soon be in the workforce earning a paycheck, able to afford marriage and the start of a life with Emilie. But I still asked God what to do about Emilie's age. Her mother surely wasn't going to give permission for her 16-year-old daughter, a high school junior, to be married. But I continued to pray that God would solve this problem in His own perfect way.

At this time I also developed a physical problem. The symptoms suggested the possibility of colon cancer, so my doctors began a series of tests to pinpoint the problem. During this process Emilie's mother met a gentleman who wanted to marry her. But Irene's suitor was not sure he wanted a teenage daughter in the arrangement. Seeing his concern I explained to Irene that I loved her daughter and that I would be graduating in a few weeks and able to take responsibility for a wife. "May I marry your daughter?" I asked her.

After discussing the matter with her fiancé, Irene responded, "I will be happy to give my consent for Emilie to marry you." God had finally solved the problem of Emilie's young age.

The final hurdle was my medical problem. I was to learn the test results on a Friday and, if the results proved negative, I planned to ask Emilie to marry me at a concert we were to attend that evening. When I met with the doctor, my heart was pounding. Many prayers had been lifted for me, so I knew God's will was being worked out for me. "You don't have cancer," the doctor announced, "but you do have a serious case of colitis." You can imagine how wonderful I felt. Now my heart was pounding with excitement. I was free to ask Emilie Klein to be my bride.

Like most couples, Emilie and I had spent many precious evenings looking at diamond rings. She had decided on a favorite, and I had returned to the store later and purchased it. On Friday evening Emilie's gleaming engagement ring, wrapped in a beautiful felt box, was hidden in my pocket as I escorted Emilie into the concert hall.

During intermission, while we were enjoying refreshments in the lobby, I summoned my courage to say, "When we get back inside I have something special to ask you."

"Oh, what is it?" she replied.

"Just wait until we are seated," I grinned.

Once back in our seats, Emilie wanted to know what was so special. "Will you marry me?" I asked shyly.

"Yes," Emilie responded confidently, "if my mother will sign for me."

"She will!" I chirped excitedly. "I've already talked to her about it!"

Almost forgetting the ring, I asked Emilie to close her eyes and hold out her hand. I pulled the box from my pocket and gently laid it on the palm of her hand. When she opened her eyes, she knew what was in the box. She anxiously lifted the lid and sighed deeply when she saw the first sparkle of light from the ring. We hugged and kissed, and I slipped the ring on her finger.

Our engagement took place in April 1955, and our wedding was set for September thirtieth. The months in between were filled with exciting plans and preparations. A few days before Emilie's mother was to sign our marriage license, her fiancé suffered a fatal heart attack. Irene was suddenly alone again, needing her daughter at home. But she had promised to sign, and she fulfilled her commitment to us.

Our wedding day began like most other days. We both went off to school—Emilie to learn, and I to teach. The ceremony was scheduled for 6:00 P.M. Because Emilie's family would not come to a Christian church for the wedding ceremony, we were married in our choir director's home. Bill and Virginia Retts had been wonderful role models for us, and they graciously opened their lovely home for our small family wedding.

> *Successful people do what unsuccessful people aren't willing to do.*

We can hardly remember the service, but we do remember saying "I do," kissing, and hearing Pastor Hubbard declare, "I pronounce you husband and wife." After the reception we took our gifts to our little apartment, opened them, and then headed for Laguna Beach for a weekend honeymoon.

Many people doubted that our marriage would succeed. But with helpful instruction from the Scriptures, our godly pastors, and many inspirational books, tapes, and speakers, we have succeeded to grow a great marriage. Most important, by allowing Jesus to be our marriage partner, we have enjoyed more than 52 years together, and we look forward to many more.

Yes, our successful marriage has required a lot of hard work. But through perseverance, love, commitment, and faithfulness, this journey has continually blessed us and, we hope, the people in our lives. Some secrets to lasting love are revealed in the freshness of new love, but many more are discovered, with delight, as a husband and wife mature in love and life together.

For the last ten years, I have had the privilege to be Emilie's caregiver during her bout with cancer. I have performed tasks that I never thought possible. I've learned how to connect bags of hydration to her catheter, give her necessary injections without fainting, and give numerous pills on an around-the-clock schedule. I've learned to cook, iron, sew, clean the house, shop—all the roles she fulfilled in our marriage. God has given me an abundance of patience while I've

There are many who want me to tell them of secret ways of becoming perfect, and I can only tell them that the sole secret is a hearty love of God, and the only way of attaining that love is by loving. You learn to speak by speaking, to study by studying, to run by running, to work by working; and just so you learn to love God and man by loving. Begin as a mere apprentice and the very power of love will lead you on to become a master of the art.

—Saint Francis of Sales

waited countless hours during her many treatments. I've been able to clean up after her many stomach disorders—accidents that have happened in bed and in the bathroom. I've called 911 at midnight because I couldn't lift her up and put her in the car to take her to the emergency room.

At the time I scratched my head and asked Him, "Are you sure this was part of the marriage vows?" He assured me that it was. I now know that it was part of "until death do us part!" I know I said it as a young groom, but did God really expect to hold me to that statement? "God, do You really expect me to go through this at my age? After all, I'm getting older, and I don't want to waste the few remaining years taking care of a sick wife." The answer came back time and time again, "Yes!"

Then I remembered a famous quote by Edward Everett Hale:

> I am only one, but I am one. I cannot do
> everything, but I can do something; and what
> I can do, that I ought to do; and what I ought
> to do, by the grace of God I shall do.

This quote, along with the many other verses in Scripture, convicted me that I needed to honor what I had promised to God, Emilie, and the many witnesses in attendance at our small homey wedding. Since then I've heard from many men who told me they were watching to see what I would do as Emilie and I walked through this valley of hardship. They've told me that I have shown them what a godly husband does when his wife becomes ill. The biggest surprise came to me from the mouths of our grandchildren. Their little eyes were watching to see how PaPa Bob was treating Grammy Emilie when she was sick.

Yes, even in the pits of life, the Lord can be glorified. I can honestly say that I am a better man and a better husband because of this trial and testing in my life.

Secrets to Romancing Your Wife

- Help your wife wash her hair.
- Cuddle up in front of a roaring fireplace (no TV, no children, and no phone).
- Bring home and watch her favorite movie.
- Write "I love you" on the bathroom mirror with a piece of soap.
- Take your wife's car to be serviced.
- Call your wife from work just to tell her you love her.
- Give your wife a kiss and thank her for all she does to make home so warm and fun.
- Write down five things you love and appreciate about your wife. Sign and date it, and then give it to her. She'll love it.

6

After the Wedding

*If any of you lacks wisdom, he should ask
God, who gives generously to all without finding
fault, and it will be given to him.*

JAMES 1:5 NIV

S omewhere between the thrill of the engagement, the hectic preparation for the wedding, and the joy of the big day—and often despite
excellent premarital counseling—the message gets lost, overlooked, or
silenced. That message? Marriage takes effort and commitment.

Genesis 2:24 states, "A man shall leave his father and his mother,
and be joined to his wife; and they shall become one flesh." Those 21
words tell it all. They sum up the complete teaching on marriage in
the Scripture. As Bob and I studied this passage, we saw that God
was calling us to:

- Departure
- Permanence
- Oneness

Departure

Besides physically leaving their parents' homes, both the husband
and wife are to become emotionally and financially independent as
well. The marriage relationship—and the new family that has been
created—is to be the primary source of emotional health, financial
provision, security, and protection for the couple.

The bonds of love for one's parents are everlasting, but these connections are to change. The new couple will not make an absolute break from their parents, but they must realize that they are now a family, and they need to make their own decisions. The new husband and wife must have greater loyalty to each other than to their parents. An early Jewish custom directed the husband to do nothing the first year of marriage except get to know his wife. That's how important total commitment was to the Jewish family. This meant the husband would not go to war, play in a baseball league, teach Sabbath school, or go on a fishing trip with the boys. Likewise the new bride was to learn about her new husband. No distractions along the way.

Physically moving from the parents' home is just one kind of necessary departure for a healthy marriage. Husbands and wives also need to depart emotionally. Too many married adults have never consciously stepped away from their parents' emotional control. The process of stepping away emotionally will be gradual, and that process is harder when strong, controlling parents are involved. In that case the departing young adult may feel guilty about leaving, but such emotional separation is necessary and healthy. It doesn't mean that we no longer care about our parents; it simply means that we are not under parental control. Adults must continue to honor their parents (see Matthew 15:3-9 and 1 Timothy 5:4-8). The new couple must continually be ready to care for them and to assume responsibility *for* them rather than responsibility *to* them.

Financial independence is another important aspect of leaving home. Leaving financially means we are free to accept financial assistance from our parents, but we no longer depend on them for the funds we need. Again, many adults have not tried to achieve financial independence because they are counting on Dad and Mom's money to be there for them.

Achieving independence from one's parents can be a long or short, easy or difficult process. One way to make the separation easier on young people as well as their parents is to follow the example of our Jewish brothers and sisters. In the Jewish wedding ceremonies Bob and I have attended, parents of both the bride and groom recite vows releasing their children from their authority. Formally releasing one's children could serve to eliminate a lot of uncertainty, guilt, and unhealthy dependence as a new couple works to get established. Again, departure doesn't mean that parents and their married children will never see each other. It does mean a new phase of the relationship has begun—one in which parents regard their children as independent adults, capable of managing their own homes, their own emotional lives, and their own financial situations.

You, as a husband, cannot freely give to your wife until you know in your heart that you are more important to her than any other person in her life. Likewise, your wife needs to know that she is the most important person in your life before she can be fully committed to you. We show our spouse that he or she holds that number one spot when, at every level, we leave our parents' house.

Permanence

According to Genesis 2:24, leaving one's father and mother is just the first step toward a strong and godly marriage. This verse states a man shall "be joined to his wife." The Hebrew word translated "joined" means "to cling" or "to be glued to" and clearly expresses God's intention that a husband and wife be bonded to one another permanently. Marriage is not an experiment or a trial run. Marriage is a once-and-for-all union. "Join" suggests determined action; there is nothing passive about this word.

In light of the fact that marriage should be permanent, God gives these instructions to a newly married couple. "When a man takes a new wife, he shall not go out with the army nor be charged with any duty; he shall be free at home one year and shall give happiness to his wife whom he has taken" (Deuteronomy 24:5). This period of time gave the couple the opportunity to get to know one another and build a foundation for a marriage that would last.

Few newlyweds have the resources that would allow them to quit their jobs and spend every moment of their first year alone together.

But there are some practical steps all married couples can take or apply to reinforce the glue of permanence in the marriage.

Leave your parents' homes and set up a home of your own. If at all possible, do not live in the same house with either of your parents—even if it is more economical to do so.

Spend as much time together as possible. Your marriage is to take priority over nights out with the boys. After all, we can't build relationships with our spouses that will last if we don't spend time together, especially when we're first married. Our spouses are more important than our friends, and our actions need to reflect that fact, even if old friends don't understand.

Reserve the bedroom for sleeping and loving. Do this by keeping the television out of your bedroom. Many husbands go to bed and watch the end of a movie, the late news, or the last play of a ball game. When this happens, the television robs many couples of the happiness they should be providing each other in the bedroom.

Permanence isn't valued in our culture today, but it's valued by our God, the One who established marriage for us. Furthermore, permanence doesn't happen automatically. It takes work—but the rewards make the work well worth the effort.

Oneness

After calling husbands and wives to leave their fathers and mothers and be joined to one another, God says that the two "shall become one flesh" (Genesis 2:24). In God's sight we become one at the altar when we say our vows to one another before Him, but practically speaking, oneness between a husband and wife is a *process* that happens over a period of time—over their lifetime together.

Becoming one can be a very hard process. It isn't easy to change from being independent and self-centered to sharing every aspect of your life and self with another person. The difficulty is intensified when you're older and more set in your ways or when the two partners come from very different family, religious, and financial backgrounds.

I came from an alcoholic family and was raised by a verbally and physically abusive father. Bob came from a warm, loving family where yelling and screaming simply didn't occur. It took us only a few moments to say our vows and enter into oneness in God's eyes, but we have spent many years blending our lives and building the oneness we enjoy today. The husband has the primary responsibility to do everything possible to ensure this bonding, to form lifelong ties with his wife. Likewise, the wife is to properly respond to her husband regarding these solidifications. They are to be taken seriously. The following Scriptures will help you grasp this concept of joining:

> *Love seeks one thing only: the good of the one loved. It leaves all the other secondary effects to take care of themselves. Love, therefore, is its own reward.*
>
> –THOMAS MERTON

- Cling to the Lord (Deuteronomy 10:20)
- Hold fast to God's ways (Deuteronomy 11:22)
- Serve God and cling to Him (Deuteronomy 13:4)
- Obey God's voice and hold fast to Him (Deuteronomy 30:20)

Becoming one doesn't mean becoming the same. Oneness means *sharing* the same degree of commitment to the Lord and to the marriage. It means having the same goals, dreams, and mission in life as a couple. The oneness and internal conformity of a marriage relationship comes with the unselfish act of allowing God to shape us into the marriage partner He would have us be. Oneness results when two individuals reflect the same Christ. Such spiritual oneness produces tremendous strength and unity in a marriage and in the family.

Consider what Paul writes to the church at Philippi: "Make my joy complete by being of the same mind, maintaining the same love, united in spirit, intent on one purpose" (Philippians 2:2). This verse has guided me in my roles as wife and mother. It has called me to work to unite my family in purpose, thought, and deed. After many years of trial, error, and endless hours of searching, I can say that Bob and I are united in our purpose and direction. If you were to ask Bob to state our purpose and direction, his answer would match mine. The litmus test for us is Matthew 6:33: "Seek first His kingdom and His righteousness, and all these things will be added to you." As we have faced decisions through the years, we've asked ourselves, "Are we seeking God's kingdom and His righteousness? Will doing this help us find His kingdom and experience His righteousness? Are we seeking our own edification or our own satisfaction?" Bob and I both hold this standard up whenever we have to decide an issue, and that oneness of purpose helps make our marriage work.

Larry Crabb pointed out another important dimension to the oneness of a husband and wife:

> The goal of oneness can be almost frightening when we realize that God does not intend [only] that my wife and I find our personal needs met in marriage. He also wants our relationship to validate the claims of Christianity to a watching world as an example of the power of Christ's redeeming love to overcome the divisive effects of sin.[1]

The world does not value permanence and oneness in a marriage, and much of our culture works to undermine those characteristics. But knowing what God intends marriage to be, working to leave our parents, joining and becoming one with our spouses, and understanding that our temperament differences can strengthen our unity with our mates—these things will help our marriages shine God's light in a very dark world.

God's pattern is monogamous: Marriage is between one man and one woman. This leaving, joining, and oneness results in a new identity in which two people become one. One in mind, heart, body, and spirit (Philippians 2:1-2). This is the pattern for a godly marriage. The blessing of these three principles is to stand before each other naked and not be ashamed (Genesis 2:24-25). Not only in physical nakedness, but also in nakedness of spirit and emotion. We are free from all guilt and shame before our mates. They are to know us as we are known by God. This foundation will stand the test of time.

Even in the best circumstances, the demands of daily life and the hours one or both spouses work outside the home take their toll on the marriage relationship. Couples become business partners, and then they become strangers. Children become the main topic of conversation and the primary focus of prayers. Elderly parents need care, bills need to be paid, the Sunday school program needs teachers, and the lawn needs to be mowed. Energy is gone from both of you long before the day is over, the day is over long before the "to do" list is complete, and the money is gone before the month ends. Even with the Lord as the foundation, marriage takes effort.

The Way of the World

Marriage is made even harder these days by the world's view of men, women, marriage, and family. What the world preaches certainly isn't what God had in mind when He made us in His image, instituted marriage, and declared it good.

The Scriptures clearly teach that God created Eve from Adam's rib, so that she could be Adam's helpmate (Genesis 2:22). Today's society, however, slams the door on that truth. While it's great that women have made important and long overdue strides toward social, political, and economic equality, some women have, unfortunately, pushed for equality to the point of ignoring the distinctive differences God created in men and women so they would complement one another. Some have even gone so far as to say, "Who needs men?" In response, many men have become passive, quiet, and unsure about their role in relation to women. In fact, they have no idea what God intends them to be, and women are frustrated because their men aren't meeting their needs in the marriage and the family. Women cry out to their husbands, "Get with the program!" and the men softly ask, "What program?" Men and women alike have strayed from God's design for marriage, and as a result, they are at odds with their mates.

> *You were running well; who hindered you from obeying the truth?*
>
> GALATIANS 5:7

As men, you need to stand up and be counted, so you can love your wife and she can accept your love. We need to dispel the lies that are given as truth. Romans 12:2 states, "Do not be conformed to this world, but be transformed by the renewing of your mind, so that you may prove what the will of God is, that which is good and acceptable and perfect." This has been and always will be the great tension we all face—that struggle of not being conformed to the world but being transformed by God. Men, you must take the leadership role and make this happen in your family. If you sit back and do nothing (as the world would like you to do), your marriage and family will fall apart. As Joshua said in chapter 24, verse 15, "But as for me and my house, we will serve the LORD."

Faithful men throughout history have had to draw a line in the sand and say, "No, I will not cross this line. I will go no further in the world's thoughts." What are some of these lies that must be rejected? Ones that will destroy your love for your wife and family.

Lie 1: You can have it all.

As a couple you must come together in agreement that life wasn't made to "have it all." There are times when we must say no. The price is too much. You and your mate may be very capable in what you do, but trying to have everything and be everything to everyone is too big of a price to pay. It may be too big of a risk and mean too many hours away from each other. The financial cost may be too great, the emotional and physical toll astronomical. Each couple has to decide when enough is enough.

As men you are the protector of your family. The trade-off of having more money is less family time. Even though the world tells us we can have it all, if you have a transformed mind, you know you can't. Your priorities are different.

Lie 2: Men and women are fundamentally the same.

Clinical studies show consistently different play patterns between young boys and girls, but we don't need sociologists and psychologists to point that out. Our own observations of the world around us and contact with members of the opposite sex reveal that males and females have different priorities, different thoughts, and different desires in life. The differences between men and women are one reason why marriage is challenging. Unfortunately many couples have refused to acknowledge these differences in their quest for liberation

He has not promised we will never be lonely. But He has promised that in Him we will never be alone. He has not promised that we will be free from pain and sorrow. But He has promised He will be our help, our strength, our everlasting peace. No matter what happens in our lives, we can believe fully in His promise. We can rest confidently in His love.

–Author Unknown

from traditional roles. Don't be misled and believe that your wife's ways are your ways, her thoughts are your thoughts, and her emotions are your emotions.

My marriage would be in a heap of trouble if I expected that my Bob would respond the same as I do. Note that different *does not* imply better or worse, superior or inferior. Acknowledging that there are differences may help you and your wife become more comfortable with your gender.

Lie 3: Men and women view sex the same way.

One basic difference between men and women is the way they approach and enjoy sex—and some of those differences are not hard to understand. First, the potential consequence of sexual intercourse—bearing a new life—has far greater ramifications in the life of a woman. In addition, the connection between sex and love is much closer and more important to women than it is to men. The sexual revolution attempted to erase this difference. In their effort to achieve equality with men, many sexually active women have tried to ignore their fundamental emotional needs. They have sacrificed their lives based on the lie that they should approach sex just as men do.

> *Take your wife out for dessert this week. Tell her how sweet your love is for her.*

If more women accepted that their Creator made them different from men, they could find wholeness, peace, and a more satisfying sexuality. Often women will ask, "How can I be more feminine?" My usual response is, "By being less masculine!" Men like the softness of a woman—her chin, her voice, her dress, her manners, her social graces, and the way she relates to them.

Men are motivated sexually by sight. Women are motivated sexually by kindness, softness, respect, and communication. For men, sex plays a large part in reflecting that his wife loves him. But for a wife, communication—talking, saying sweet words in her ears and heart—is a big stimulus for her to be sexually engaged.

Lie 4: Speaking your mind is better than listening.

Men and women alike miss out on the bond that compassionate listening can forge between them. One way in which a woman feels loved is when her husband puts down the newspaper, turns off the TV, and gives her his full attention. And, men, she doesn't always expect or want you to solve the problems she mentions. She just wants to know that you care enough to listen.

Men, remember that women speak approximately 25,000 words a day, and men usually speak half of her total: 12,500. A woman's love gauge needs to talk, talk, talk and have you listen, listen, listen. Yes, I know men want just the facts, to get to the bottom line, to not hear every detail—but women must talk it out.

In the New Testament, James instructs believers to be "quick to hear, slow to speak" (James 1:19). In today's culture of busyness, many of us are more comfortable doing instead of being; consequently, we like to speak instead of listening.

Scripture tells us that our speech is to be kind to the hearer. One of the greatest speech guidelines is found in Ephesians 4:29: "Let no unwholesome word proceed from your mouth, but only such a word as is good for edification according to the need of the moment, so that it will give grace to those who hear." A guiding principle in our family is: You never have to apologize for words you never say.

Any words spoken need to be covered in love. Am I saying a couple can never argue? No. You can argue, but you need to set ground rules when you do. One of them is you don't attack the other person with hurtful dialog.

One of the ways Bob and I have filled our speech with love is in the careful choice of words we use with each other. We like the two lists Denis Waitley has in his book *Seeds of Greatness Treasury*. He shares what words we should forget and what words we should remember in loving conversation.

Words to Forget	Words to Remember
I can't	I can
I'll try	I will
I have to	I want to
I should have	I will do
I could have	My goal
Someday	Today
If only	Next time
Yes, but	I understand
Problem	Opportunity
Difficult	Challenging
Stressed	Motivated
Worried	Interested
Impossible	Possible
I, me, my	You, your
Hate	Love[2]

I can do everything God asks me to with the help of Christ who gives me the strength and power.

PHILIPPIANS 4:13 TLB

Are there some words in your vocabulary you need to forget and replace with words that affirm your love and deepen your intimacy? Consciously watch your language. Communicate using positive, loving words. If your words are not edifying, switch gears in your mind and your mouth and begin to speak only words worth remembering. Negative words kill the spirit; positive words build up your mate.

Challenging These Lies

Consider the impact that these and other lies have on our society. When we believe in and act on these lies, we not only undermine society, but we also find ourselves living contrary to God's plan. When we try to redesign the plan He instituted in the beginning, our efforts dishonor the Creator. Despite that fact and despite the negative consequences of these lies, they still influence much of today's thinking about men and women.

Secrets to Romancing Your Marriage

- Write each other a poem.
- Hold each other's hand as you walk together.
- Turn off the TV, listen to some soft music, and talk together.
- Join an exercise class together.
- Say "I'm sorry" when it's appropriate.
- Subscribe to his favorite sports magazine.
- Make her a fresh cup of tea while she is watching TV.

7

Simple Secrets
Every Wife Should Know

Her children stand and bless her; so does her husband.
He praises her with these words:
"There are many fine women in the world,
but you are the best of them all!"

PROVERBS 31:28-29 TLB

You've already discovered that my family background was very different from Bob's. Bob grew up under his father's excellent model of a Christian husband. But I didn't know what it meant to be a Christian—let alone a Christian wife—until I was 17 years old. Up to my conversion, I gave very little thought to the biblical requirements for being a godly wife.

Even though I didn't know the difference between my home and a Christian home, I knew there were problems in my family that I didn't want repeated when I married. My alcoholic father was abusive to my mother and brother, often screaming at them, swearing at them, and hitting them. I knew that I didn't want to marry a man like my father.

After Daddy died of an alcohol-induced heart attack when I was 11 years old, our home life was better for a while. But my brother, Edmund, was in junior high school and soon began to test Mom's boundaries. Again our home became a battleground, this time between a rebellious teenager and a physically and emotionally weary mother.

When I was home alone, I pretended that our apartment was a cute white house with a picket fence. I imagined that I was a wife and mother waiting for my husband to arrive home from work. I would clean, vacuum, and cook a delicious dinner as if for him. But often when Mom and Edmund arrived home, the fantasy was shattered. Dinner usually ended with somebody crying and doors being slammed. I would run to my bed, bury my face in my pillow, and sob, wishing I could have a normal family.

I had several girlfriends who would invite me to their homes after school to do homework and practice musical instruments. I loved being asked by their mothers to stay for dinner, and I added many of their recipes to my collection. I also enjoyed getting to know my friends' fathers, who were always warm and friendly to me. I would go home after those visits and lie in bed thinking about my future husband and children. Happy memories from those positive families helped keep me going.

Soon after I met Bob, I realized that he possessed the qualities I had dreamed about in a husband—qualities which were missing in my home. When he began taking me to his church, I discovered what God had to say in the Bible about marriage and being a godly wife. These truths were entirely new and refreshing to me. I became aware that God had a plan for me as a woman in His design for marriage. As Bob shared his faith in Christ with me, I could see that he had something that I wanted for my life.

Bob's family made a great impact on my life at this time. I just loved going to their home. I remember wondering if Bob would grow up to be as nice as his father. His mother, Gertie, was a great southern cook who introduced me to many new recipes. They both showered me with love and made me feel like a member of the family. There were always lots of hugs, laughter, and good manners. Mealtime prayers were a wonderful new experience for me.

After several months of hearing God's Word preached and seeing it lived in Bob and his family, I came to know Jesus as my Lord and Savior. Then I started thinking about being a Christian wife. When

Bob and I were married, neither of us knew much of what the Bible said about being a Christian husband and wife. But we did want to learn. So we attended young married couples' Bible studies and committed ourselves to be what God wanted us to be. We learned as we grew—we are still learning to apply biblical principles to our marriage.

The Model Wife

One of the first passages of Scripture on the topic of the Christian wife that caught my attention was Proverbs 31:10-31.

> If you can find a truly good wife, she is worth more than precious gems! Her husband can trust her, and she will richly satisfy his needs. She will not hinder him but help him all her life. She finds wool and flax and busily spins it. She buys imported foods brought by ship from distant ports. She gets up before dawn to prepare breakfast for her household and plans the day's work for her servant girls. She goes out to inspect a field and buys it; with her own hands she plants a vineyard. She is energetic, a hard worker, and watches for bargains. She works far into the night!

> She sews for the poor and generously helps those in need. She has no fear of winter for her household, for she has made warm clothes for all of them. She also upholsters with finest tapestry; her own clothing is beautifully made—a purple gown of pure linen. Her husband is well known, for he sits in the council chamber with the other civic leaders. She makes belted linen garments to sell to the merchants.

> She is a woman of strength and dignity and has no fear of old age. When she speaks, her words are wise, and kindness is the rule for everything she says. She watches carefully all that goes on throughout her household and is never lazy. Her children stand and bless her; so does her husband. He praises her with these words: "There are many fine women in the world, but you are the best of them all!"

Charm can be deceptive and beauty doesn't last, but a woman who fears and reverences God shall be greatly praised. Praise her for the many fine things she does. Those good deeds of hers shall bring her honor and recognition from people of importance (TLB).

I have listened to others teach on this passage and have taught from it myself for more than 35 years, but I am continually learning new principles from these verses. The woman described here has been the model for my life. In fact, I have fashioned my seminar, "More Hours in My Day," from what this passage says to today's woman.

As I have studied Proverbs 31:10-31, I have identified 15 characteristics of a godly wife. I remember listing these characteristics on paper once and then writing, next to each trait, ways I would develop that trait in my life. At first I thought it would be a four-to-six-week project, but I have discovered that it is a lifetime assignment.

The 15 characteristics are listed and described on the left below. As you read each one, jot down one or two ways by which you can incorporate it into your life (see the example for the first one).

The Godly Wife Is...

CHARACTERISTIC	ACTION
1. Valuable (v. 10): She has value which increases with time.	Example: Take a cooking class Go back to college
2. Trustworthy (v. 11a): She is reliable, consistent, secure; she can be counted on.	_____ _____ _____ _____
3. Willing to satisfy his needs (v. 11b): She is understanding; she knows what makes him tick.	_____ _____ _____ _____

4. A helpmate (v. 12): She
doesn't hinder him but
encourages and praises
him.

_____
_____
_____
_____

5. Industrious (vv. 13-14,18):
She is hard-working,
diligent, active, busy,
and persistent.

_____
_____
_____
_____

6. Well-organized (v. 15):
She plans ahead, shares,
and gives of herself.

_____
_____
_____

7. Good in business (v. 16):
She knows a good bargain
and invests wisely.

_____
_____
_____

8. Energetic (vv. 17-18): She is
never lazy and often works
long hours.

_____
_____
_____

9. Compassionate (vv. 19-20):
She is tenderhearted,
responsive, warm, and
willing to help.

_____
_____
_____
_____

10. Domestic (vv. 21-22,25):
She is a seamstress and a
designer; she is color
conscious.

_____
_____
_____
_____

11. Aware of who she is (v. 25):
She has an inner peace, good
self-esteem, and is physically
sound.

_____
_____
_____

12. Kind (v. 26): She speaks with wisdom and kindness.

_____
_____

13. Observant (v. 27): She watches what goes on and pays attention to detail.

_____
_____
_____

14. Blessed (vv. 23,28-29): Her children bless her and her husband praises her.

_____
_____
_____

15. Spiritual (v. 30): She has the inner quality of reverence for God.

_____
_____
_____

> *In the long run men hit only what they aim at. Therefore, though they should fail immediately, they had better aim at something high.*
>
> –HENRY DAVID THOREAU

I have met many women who didn't want to work this hard on their marriages until it was too late. Let me encourage you. Now is the time—before your marriage is in trouble—to become the person God wants you to be. And even if you are already experiencing marriage problems, it's never too late to become the person God wants you to be. Circumstances and relationships may fall apart, and perhaps they cannot be restored. But if you are open to change, God can make a new person out of you.

Recently I received the following letter.

Dear Emilie,

This is an update of my recent letter asking you for help.

Evidently I have sought help too late because last Thursday my husband told me he wanted a divorce. I cannot describe the empty, sick feeling I felt at that shock. I have barely been able to eat.

I realize now my priorities were way off base. I have offended him to the point that I have destroyed God's work in his life and our family relationship. It grieves me to expose the children to this traumatic experience at their vulnerable ages.

I have asked him to let us try to work it out, assuring him that, with the Lord's will in my life, I can change. He feels it is too late. He has agreed to pastoral consultation for my benefit but stated that his ears are closed.

Your tapes, books, and seminars are a blessing to me at this time, but I fear that I have heard them too late.

Sincerely,

Shirley

This lady knew that her priorities were out of proper order, and she was grieving to restore the damage she had caused her husband and children. Ladies, you know when things aren't right in your relationships. Please don't wait until it's too late. Confess your shortcomings to God and move into a positive position in life.

Bob uses a phrase that is a good reminder to those of us striving to be godly women, "No pain, no gain." It will cost you something to become a Proverbs 31 woman—time, energy, prayer, and discipline to name just a few. But the inestimable gain, which follows the pain, is the blessing and praise of your family.

The Balancing Act

Life is hectic for women today. We hear so many voices trying to redefine the role of wives, mothers, and women in society and the church. In the meantime we get tired of cooking, shopping, laundering, cleaning, ironing, and being a taxi driver who takes the kids to little league games, music lessons, and church and school activities. Recently I was talking with a woman whose husband plays baseball for the California Angels. She said that, between the baseball activities of her husband and their sons, she attends up to 15 baseball games a week!

At age 21, with five children under the age of five, I was ready to give up on motherhood. I was bored and burned out. I cried, "Stop! I want off!" Sometimes, when Bob was at school, I would weep from frustration and fatigue. At that point in my "career," my motivations were all wrong. True, I wanted to be a helpmate for Bob, but I was caught up in the pressure of trying to meet everyone's expectations— including my own. The house always had to be perfect and the children spotless. I was frustrated as a wife and mother because I was doing it all myself—100 percent from me and nothing from God. I was trying to be the phantom wife Dennis Rainey expected his wife Barbara to be, as described in the book *Building Your Mate's Self-Esteem*:

> She is the perfect wife, mother and friend, always loving, patient, understanding and kind. She is well-organized, with a perfect balance between being disciplined and flexible. Her house is always neat and well-decorated, and her children obey the first time, every time. She is serious yet lighthearted, submissive but not passive. She is energetic and never tired. She looks fresh and attractive at all times whether in jeans and a sweater digging in her garden or in a silk dress and heels going out to dinner. She never gets sick, lonely or discouraged. And because her phantom is a Christian, Dennis sees her faithfully walking with God daily. This phantom prays regularly, studies diligently and is not fearful or inhibited about sharing her faith or speaking the truth to someone who may be in error.[1]

During this time in my life, I came across Philippians 1:6: "And I am sure that God who began the good work within you will keep right on helping you grow in his grace until his task within you is finally finished on that day when Jesus Christ returns" (TLB). I realized that I was the product of God working in me and that I had three alternatives for solving my dilemma:

1. I could keep trying to be super-wife and super-mom by doing everything myself, or
2. I could follow the old adage, "Let go and let God," and let God do everything, or
3. I could enter a balanced partnership with God.

I selected the last alternative knowing that, according to Philippians 2:12-13, God was at work inside me, helping me to obey Him and to do what He wanted. God had made me a wife and a mom on purpose, and He would help me perform my role. Once I accepted this truth, a burden was lifted. I was less stressed, and homemaking became a real joy when I saw myself as a partner with God in developing godly traits in my children and creating a warm, safe nest for our family.

As I searched the Scriptures to discover my role in the partnership, I came up with three areas:

Faithfulness. According to 1 Corinthians 4:2, if I am to be a good manager of my home, I must remain faithful. Specifically, God wants me to faithfully thank Him for fulfilling His plans in my family. I'm often impatient, wanting things to change "right now." But God wants me to stop being concerned about His timetable and just give thanks. Through the years I have learned that if I am faithful in giving thanks, God is faithful in His part.

Obedience. It is my responsibility to act upon God's promises for my life. I can't just sit back and do nothing. Nor can I wait until all situations are perfect and safe. I must do a good job of preparation and then move ahead obediently, even if it means risking failure. Some of my best steps of growth have come after failure.

Growth. When Bob and I attended Bill Gothard's seminar

years ago, he was distributing badges with the following initials: P.B.P.G.I.N.F.W.M.Y. I soon found out that the letters represented the simple message, "Please be patient; God is not finished with me yet." Yes, the Christian walk is a process of growth. I wanted to arrive instantly at the level of being a perfect wife and mother. But God showed me that my focus was to be on the lifelong process. If we focus on perfection, we'll always be disappointed. But if we focus on the process of growth, we can always have hope for improvement tomorrow.

Goal Setting and Priority Planning

In Psalm 90:12 the psalmist prays, "Teach us to number our days and recognize how few they are; help us to spend them as we should" (TLB). When I read this verse I realized that God has given me only so many days to carry out His plans in my life. I decided that I needed to prioritize the various areas of my life to maximize my efficiency as a Proverbs 31 woman for the days God has given me.

Priority #1: God. Matthew 6:33 says, "Seek first his kingdom and his righteousness, and all these things will be given to you as well" (NIV). This verse helped me understand that, in all my responsibilities, God was to be first. He challenged me early in my married life to eliminate some of my activities and develop a deeper walk with Him.

I knew that if God was to be first in my life, I needed to talk with Him more. He encouraged me to get up at 5:30 each morning for Bible reading and prayer. The early hour was difficult at first, but soon I began to enjoy getting up to talk to and listen to Him for 30 uninterrupted minutes.

Shortly after starting these early morning devotions, I became frustrated because I couldn't get through all my prayer requests in one morning. I needed to organize my time in order to be more efficient and effective. So I purchased a small three-ring notebook and divided the pages into the following sections for daily prayer:

- Monday: Family—I keep a page for each family member, complete with a picture.

- Tuesday: Church—I pray for our pastors and their families, youth leaders, elders, deacons, music director, and others.
- Wednesday: Personal—I pray for my daily schedule, meal planning, cleaning, relationships, weaknesses, and goals.
- Thursday: Finances—I pray about our budget, expenses, purchases, and tithing.
- Friday: Illnesses—I pray for relatives and friends who are ill or caring for the ill.
- Saturday: Government—I pray for the president, governor, congress, senators, local officials, and others in position of leadership.
- Sunday: Sermon notes/outlines—I outline each sermon and write down prayer requests from the church body to be transferred to the appropriate pages in my notebook.

For each request in my notebook, I write down the date it was entered and the date it was answered. God always answers prayer in one of three ways: yes, no, or wait.

I don't get up at 5:30 A.M. these days because I now have other blocks of time for prayer that are more convenient to my schedule. One time of day is no more spiritual than another. You just need to find a block of time that is good for you. Be flexible, but be consistent.

Priority #2: Husband. One evening Bob said to me, "You love the children more than you love me. I feel like all I'm good for is a paycheck." His revelation came as a complete shock to me. He was telling me that he didn't feel needed, appreciated, or loved as he would like. I loved and respected Bob deeply, but somehow it wasn't getting through to him.

Bob's confrontation helped me realize that I was a wife to my husband before I was a mother to my children. Proverbs 12:4 states, "A worthy wife is her husband's joy and crown; the other kind corrodes his strength and tears down everything he does" (TLB).

I knew I wanted to be Bob's joy and crown. I wanted to lift him up.

So for a while I focused on the area of making sure Bob was aware of his importance to me. I even helped the children invest in Dad's stock. As a team we lifted Bob to his proper position in our family.

Through the years I have assured Bob that he is a priority by mailing love messages to him, placing special "love baskets" for him to find, preparing his favorite foods, and occasionally kidnapping him for a romantic weekend. We continue our romance even after all these years.

If you are aware that your husband has not been a priority in your life, you may want to make special plans by which you will honor him this week. For example, you may decide to faithfully greet him at the door with a kiss or send him a love note at work.

> *I was a wife to my husband before I was a mother to my children.*

Priority #3: Children. Deuteronomy 6:4-7 instructs us that our ministry to our children is to be a priority in our lives: "Jehovah is our God, Jehovah alone. You must love him with all your heart, soul, and might. And you must think constantly about these commandments I am giving you today. You must teach them to your children and talk about them when you are at home or out for a walk; at bedtime and the first thing in the morning" (TLB). We are to use every opportunity to teach our children about God.

We found vacation time to be an excellent time to teach our children about God and His marvelous creation. While in the desert, at the ocean, in the mountains, or beside a river, we discussed God's handiwork in nature. Many times we conducted our own church services as a family, with each member taking responsibility for part of the service. Vacations together were great times for us.

Another way I made our children a priority was to be available to them. As very young children they posed the most wonderful, penetrating questions. That's one of the reasons I decided to stay home with them instead of hold a job. I wanted to be there to answer their questions.

Many child psychologists agree that one of the most important things a mother can do for her child is to love the child's father, and the most important thing a father can do for his child is to love the child's mother.

A child can be loved by the mother and loved by the father, but if Mommy and Daddy don't love each other, a child can have a deep feeling of insecurity. We committed ourselves to teach our children about love by being parents who loved one another.

Your husband must be a priority over your children because eventually your children will grow up and depart, leaving the two of you alone again. If your children have been your priority, their departure may leave you with many unanswered questions about your relationship with your husband. But if you have kept your husband as a priority during the child-rearing years, your love, romance, and friendship will continue to grow even in the empty-nest period of your lives.

Tell about the first time you knew you were in love with your husband.

Priority #4: Home. As a young girl, I dreamed about having a home that was neat, well organized, and filled with the fragrances of cooking and baking, the sounds of soothing music, and the spoken language of love. I wanted to decorate it with frilly ribbons, bows and straw, and pictures to match the décor. I wanted my home to be a place my friends wanted to visit.

Through the years Bob and I have been blessed to live in homes that have fulfilled my childhood dreams. But I discovered early that dreams don't make a house a home. It takes planning, organization, resourcefulness, and elbow grease to make your home a warm and welcome haven for your family and friends. That's why a godly wife "watches carefully all that goes on throughout her household and is never lazy" (Proverbs 31:27 TLB).

Even though I have a good handle on organization, I continue to be a learner in this area. I look for easier ways to complete household jobs. I read books and newspaper articles on the subject. Many of the tips I have discovered and practiced are explained in detail in four of my books, *More Hours in My Day, Emilie's Creative Home Organizer, 15 Minute Organizer,* and *Cleaning Up the Clutter.*

Around our home we have annual mottoes to help keep the priority of our home in perspective. One year our motto was, "Don't put it down, put it away." The next was, "File it, don't pile it." And then there was, "Do less and reduce stress." Our mottoes have been enjoyable ways to involve the whole family in caring for the home. I challenge you to work hard to make your home an inviting place for those who live there and those who visit.

Priority 5: Yourself. Many women come to our seminars crying out, "Does a wife and mother ever get time for herself?" Yes, but it seldom happens by accident. Priority time for yourself must be planned and appropriated to prevent burnout.

When our children were young, I found that the more organized I was in my housework, the more time I was able to carve out for myself. Also, our neighborhood mothers developed a babysitting co-op so that each woman could have an occasional morning or afternoon to "do her own thing."

Review your schedule and discover time slots that you can claim as your own.

Priority 6: Outside the Home. At this stage you may be saying, "I can't juggle another ball. The first five priorities take more time than I have." If so, don't add another commitment. Each time you are asked to take an outside-the-home responsibility, you have three possible responses: Yes, no, or maybe. Concentrate only on the yes responses. Wait for a different season in your life to chair the PTA, teach a Sunday school class, serve as a den mother, head up a charity fund-raising committee, or lead a woman's Bible study group. Your responsibilities to God, your husband, your children, your home, and yourself are higher priorities at this time.

Leave the Changing to God

Many women I meet at our seminars ask me how they can change their husbands. I gently remind them that the Holy Spirit, not the wife, is the change agent. Our scriptural role is very clear, "Be subject to one another in the fear of Christ. Wives, be subject to your own husbands, as to the Lord...and the wife must see to it that she respects her husband" (Ephesians 5:21-22,33). We are to respect our husbands, not seek to change them.

Whenever I tried to change Bob, I provoked tension, discouragement, and resistance in him, and I hindered God's work in his life. Many times I found that my responses to Bob's shortcomings were worse than his shortcomings. We need to be sensitive to our verbal and nonverbal messages to our husbands and confess our improper responses. Then we must support our husbands in prayer and be prepared to wait for the Holy Spirit to do His work.

One main reason why we want our husbands to change is because we are self-centered. We want our men to fit our ideals for the perfect husband. Instead, we need to apply the wisdom of Philippians 2:3-4 to our relationships with our husbands: "Do nothing from selfishness or empty conceit, but with humility of mind regard one another as more important than yourselves; do not merely look out for your own personal interests, but also for the interests of others." This is impossible to do over a long period of time without being subject to one another in the fear (reverence) of God. I continually pray for guidance in this area. Satan always wants to attack me here. And I find that this is an area where most women are vulnerable.

Instead of changing your mate, you need to concentrate on what God wants from you. First Peter 3:1-2 tells women how to live with an unresponsive mate: "Wives, fit in with your husbands' plans; for then if they refuse to listen when you talk to them about the Lord, they will be won by your respectful, pure behavior. Your godly lives will speak to them better than any words" (TLB). Is this easy to do? Not until you come to grips with the fact that God designed marriage relationships to work best this way.

Wives, God wants us to respect our husbands. Maybe he doesn't deserve your respect, but that doesn't matter. God does not say your husband has earned the right to be your head or deserves it. He says that He, God, decided this was the best plan and therefore asks you to honor the plan. Speak respectfully of him in private and in public and teach your children to do the same. Accept him at face value and trust God for any needed changes. Submit to his authority in God's chain of command (see 1 Corinthians 11:3). Build his self-image by showing approval and admiration.

Greet your husband at the door with a hug and a kiss. Tell him you're glad he is home and give him space to unwind from work and his commute home. Tell him you love him in many creative ways. Step out of the way and let him take the lead God ordained for him. Don't continually nag, remind, belittle, or embarrass your husband. Aim for that quiet and gentle spirit that will prompt your husband to say, "There are many fine women in the world, but you are the best of them all!" (Proverbs 31:29 TLB).

Secrets to Romancing Your Husband

≟ Write your husband a thank-you note just for being himself. Place it under his pillow.

≟ Fly a kite together.

≟ Wash and vacuum his car until it sparkles like new.

≟ Reorganize his sock and underwear drawer.

≟ Wash and iron his dress shirts that need attention.

- Give him a shoulder, neck, and back rub.
- Shine his dress shoes.
- Run an errand for him today.
- Take his clothes to the cleaners.
- Surprise him with tickets to a game or a movie that he'll enjoy.

8

Simple Secrets Every Husband Should Know

*Husbands, love your wives, just as Christ also
loved the church and gave Himself for her.*

EPHESIANS 5:25 NKJV

When it came to learning how to be a good husband, I had a good role model in my father. Dad was a God-fearing man who wanted to do what the Scriptures taught. His generation had even less teaching in the area of family life than I did. But Dad's example provided some valuable lessons that got me off to a good start.

For example, Dad loved his wife—something my brothers and I never doubted for one moment. He surprised Mom with flowers and an occasional box of candy, and he kissed and hugged her in front of us.

Furthermore, Dad took his family to church. He was not one to drop us off and return home to drink another cup of coffee and read the Sunday paper. He was the leader of our spiritual pack Sunday morning, Sunday evening, and Wednesday evening for prayer meeting. Dad prayed at our meals, prayed alone, and read his Bible faithfully. He was a deacon or trustee for many of his years, and he regularly gave of his money and his time to the church. I am grateful to God for the example of a spiritual husband and father He provided for me in my dad.

Sadly many men enter into marriage with little or no positive role models from their past. And often new believers have little knowledge of the scriptural guidelines for the husband's role in marriage. This generation of Christian husbands is bombarded with opportunities to learn these truths through Christian marriage seminars, videos, tapes, and books. Yet we still find many men asking, "What is my role in marriage?"

Sometimes the husband's role is clouded by the unrealistic expectations his wife brings into the relationship. Barbara Rainey, coauthor with her husband of *Building Your Mate's Self-Esteem,* describes the phantom husband she projected on Dennis:

> He rises early, has a quiet time reading the Bible and praying, and then jogs several seven-minute miles. After breakfast with his family, he presents a fifteen-minute devotional. Never forgetting to hug and kiss his wife good-bye, he arrives at work ten minutes early. He is consistently patient with his co-workers, always content with his job, and has problem-solving techniques for every situation. At lunch he eats only perfectly healthy foods. His desk is never cluttered, and he is confidently in control. He arrives home on time every day and never turns down his boys when they want to play catch.
>
> His phantom is well-read in world events, politics, key issues of our day, the Scriptures and literary classics. He's a handyman around the house and loves to build things for his wife. He is socially popular and never tires of people or of helping them in time of need. He obeys all traffic laws and never speeds, even if he's late. He can quote large sections of Scripture in a single bound, has faith more powerful than a locomotive, and is faster than a speeding bullet in solving family conflicts... He also keeps his garage neat. He never loses things, always flosses his teeth and has no trouble with his weight. And he has time to fish.[1]

Men, as hard as we might try, we probably won't be able to fulfill all of our wives' expectations for us, especially if they are as lofty as

Barbara Rainey's. But we do have a standard to shoot for, which, if diligently pursued, will help us to honor God and please our wives. Let's turn to God's Word and see what He has to say on the important topic of the husband's role in marriage.

The Submissive Husband

In his letter to the church at Ephesus, Paul gave some profound instruction on how we are to serve Christ in our various relationships. A key verse on this topic is Ephesians 5:21: "Be subject to one another in the fear of Christ." This verse really caught my eye because it comes *before* the specific instructions to wives and husbands beginning in verse 22. The first instruction to husbands and wives is to adopt a spirit of mutual submission to one another out of reverence for Christ. A Christian husband and wife each have Christ living in them. In order to reverence Christ we must reverence the vessel He dwells in. When we submit to one another, we are submitting to Christ. That's the only way verses 22 and 25 can make sense. Without an attitude of mutual submission, the husband becomes the big boss, and the wife becomes the doormat. But the priority of mutual submission keeps the specific instructions to husbands and wives in proper perspective.

Paul teaches husbands about their role in Ephesians 5:25-30:

> Husbands, love your wives, just as Christ loved the church and gave himself up for her to make her holy, cleansing her by the washing with water through the word, and to present her to himself as a radiant church, without stain or wrinkle or any other blemish, but holy and blameless. In this same way, husbands ought to love their wives as their own bodies. He who loves his wife loves himself. After all, no one ever hated his own body, but he feeds and cares for it, just as Christ does the church—for we are members of his body (NIV).

My first response to this instruction was, "Oh, that's easy—as long as she promises to love me first, wash my clothes, cook great meals, and always look pretty." Then I remembered verse 21 and reminded myself that I can't act on the basis of such promises. Loving Emilie had to start with submitting to her and to the Lord. Once I grasped that principle, I began to submit to Christ in a fresh, new way. Even though Ephesians 5:22 states that Emilie was to be submissive to me, I knew I was subject to a higher calling—*mutual submission*. I began to realize that I was not to control or dominate Emilie, but I was to humbly and sacrificially love her. I was to set aside my rights and serve her needs.

> *Never let loyalty and kindness get away from you! Wear them like a necklace; write them on your heart.*

Fortunately I was raised in a home which taught and modeled sacrificial love through kindness and good manners. So during our courtship, I graciously opened the car door for Emilie, assisted her with her chair when being seated at the dining table, allowed her to go through the doorway ahead of me, and performed other kind acts I had learned as a boy. But Paul's instructions helped me see that the motivation for such kindness to Emilie was humble submission to Jesus in her.

I heard a true story about a man whose wife had always wanted him to open the car door for her. But instead of complying, he would always make fun of her request with remarks like, "What's wrong with your own two hands? Are they broken?" And he refused to open the car door for her.

The man's wife passed away before he did. At her funeral he was preceding the pallbearers as they carried her casket to the hearse. Because the man was the first to arrive at the hearse, the funeral director asked him to open the door so the pallbearers could slide the casket inside. As the man reached for the door handle, he remembered his wife's persistent request. He sadly realized that the only time he had fulfilled her wish was at her funeral.

At first glance manners may seem to be a small area of submission. But manners are a very practical way to show our reverence for Christ by serving our mates.

Submissive Leadership

Another area where I learned submission was in my role as the leader in our home. I found that when I led out of respect for Christ and for my wife, Emilie was eager to follow.

Through the years of our ministry, we have found that women are eager to follow their husbands' lead in attending church, praying and reading the Bible together, giving, attending couples' retreats, and so forth. Our wives are just waiting for us to take responsibility for spiritual leadership in our homes. Our children are also looking for spiritual direction and leadership. They feel more secure when we place boundaries around them. Recently our daughter, Jenny, said to me, "Dad, I thought you were too strict when Brad and I were growing up. But now I appreciate the direction you provided for our lives. Bill and I are going to be even tougher on our four children."

Jesus doesn't lead the church as a harsh dictator. He leads by taking initiative, by loving, and by serving. This is the pattern of leadership we men need to follow in leading our families. Take a few moments to jot down some leadership steps you need to put into motion in three areas:

Taking Initiative	Loving	Serving
1. _____	1. _____	1. _____
2. _____	2. _____	2. _____
3. _____	3. _____	3. _____

They say it takes 21 days to establish a new habit. Stick with your new steps of leadership until they become second nature. And remember, your goal is not to change your mate; it's to change you. Ask yourself, "Would I like being married to me?" If you cannot answer with a wholehearted yes, what changes do you need to make in you? List some of them here:

Changes in Me

1. _____

2. _____

3. _____

4. _____

I would like to tell you that our marriage has always been heavenly, but I can't because it hasn't. Whenever I strayed from the instructions in Ephesians 5:25-30, I have experienced marital problems. No, we have never talked about getting a divorce; the word has never been in our vocabulary. When I committed myself "for richer or for poorer, in sickness and in health," I meant it. However, there were times when my pursuit of success wrongfully took priority over my growth as a Christian. I put God on hold for several years. We didn't stop going through the motions of a wonderful family. But in my heart I knew that I wasn't the spiritual husband and father I was supposed to be.

My turning point was in 1967 when we moved to Newport Beach, California, and began attending Mariners Church. At that time I got involved with a group of men who began to challenge me to fulfill my role as a Christian husband and father. I experienced a new awareness that my first responsibility, after serving God, is to serve my wife. I have endeavored to fulfill that responsibility ever since.

Unconditional Love

Our submissive, serving love for our wives is to be unconditional and committed to giving, not getting. The focus is to be her heart's desires, not ours. Consequently I can never view my wife as an instrument of my pleasure or convenience, such as my nurse, servant, dishwasher, cook, or errand girl. I can never ask her to do something degrading or harmful to fulfill my whims or wishes. She is my helpmate and my partner. We are a team with similar goals and desires. I must continually love her and serve her for who she is, not what she can do for me.

The Responsible Husband

Another passage of Scripture that has given me direction for my role as a husband is 1 Peter 3:7: "You husbands in the same way, live with your wives in an understanding way, as with someone weaker, since she is a woman; and show her honor as a fellow heir of the grace of life, so that your prayers will not be hindered." Peter clearly states here that husbands must perform two responsibilities and, in return, will receive one specific reward.

Responsibility #1: We are to live with our wives in an understanding way. The King James Version of 1 Peter 3:7 says we are to "dwell with them according to knowledge." Knowledge of what? The knowledge of wives and marriage, of course. We need to find out why wives are weird and husbands are strange.

Learning to live with our wives in an understanding way is more on-the-job training than anything else. Seminars, books, and tapes are great, but there is no substitute for patient, observant, day-to-day living with a wife to expand your knowledge of her. Even in my fifth decade with Emilie, I am still learning about her. Our marriage relationship is always in process.

What are some areas you want to better understand about your mate and your marriage? Write some of your questions below, and then decide on how you will start finding the answers to each:

Questions I Have	How I Will Find Answers
1. _____	1. _____
2. _____	2. _____
3. _____	3. _____
4. _____	4. _____
5. _____	5. _____

Responsibility #2: We are to grant our wives honor as fellow heirs of the grace of God. One of the ways we can honor our wives is by being respectful and courteous, and by employing good manners, as we have already discussed. Another way to honor them is by openly communicating our appreciation for who they are and what they do. Tell your wife that you like her new hairstyle, that you enjoyed the recipe she tried for dinner, that the house looks neat, or that the children are responding well to her training. Thank her for ironing your shirts and fixing your sack lunches. Express your appreciation in conversation, in notes and cards, and through special treats like dinner out or a getaway weekend.

Honor your wife by speaking favorably of her to others. She is not your "old lady." She has a name, and she has the important role of being your wife and the mother of your children. Your respectful words about her will fulfill Ephesians 4:29 by edifying all who hear you. We must also teach our children to honor their mothers with respectful talk and behavior. If children are discourteous or impolite to their mothers, they will carry the problem into their marriage relationships by being disrespectful to their mates.

Peter described our wives as fellow heirs of the grace of life. That means that our wives are to be equal recipients of the gifts God has for us. The current women's liberation movement is two thousand years behind the times. God gave women a position of spiritual equality when He gave us the New Testament. I know that many husbands are threatened by their wives' spiritual growth. But my prayer over the years has been that Emilie would become the woman that God wants her to be. I am not threatened by her growth or her spiritual gifts, even in the areas where she outshines me.

The honor we show our wives is like an investment, such as the investments Emilie and I have made in stocks, bonds, mutual funds, certificates of deposit, and treasury bonds. Through the years we have watched our stocks increase in value and enjoyed the dividends that our investments have returned. Similarly as you invest daily in your wife by honoring her in word and deed, you will see her sense of self-worth increase. Furthermore, you will reap dividends in your marriage that greatly exceed your initial investment.

The reward: Our prayers will not be hindered. Peter suggests that our relationships with our wives correlate directly to our relationship with God. If you fail to understand and honor your wife, your prayers will be hindered, but if your horizontal relationship with your wife is in harmony, your vertical relationship with God will also be in harmony. You cannot ignore God's principles for marriage and expect to grow in your relationship with God.

List below what you are already doing to fulfill each responsibility. Then list a few areas where you are lacking and what you can do to improve those areas:

Understanding My Wife

I Am Doing	*I Am Lacking*	*I Will Do*
1. Showing kindness	1. Patience	1. Practice patience
2. _____	2. _____	2. _____
3. _____	3. _____	3. _____

Honoring My Wife

I Am Doing	*I Am Lacking*	*I Will Do*
1. Compliment her	1. Courtesy	1. Open car door
2. _____	2. _____	2. _____
3. _____	3. _____	3. _____

The Manager in the Home

As Emilie and I travel the country speaking at seminars, we hear a lot of women asking this question, "How can I get my husband involved in the home? He is so passive." It is clear to us that many Christian husbands have not accepted the spiritual responsibility of being the leaders in their homes.

First Timothy 3:1-3 contains a list of specific qualifications that Paul instructed Timothy to look for in church leaders. I believe any man who is seeking God's will in his life should use this list as a guideline whether or not he is a pastor, elder, or other church leader. The qualifications here outline the characteristics God is looking for in all Christian men.

Look particularly at verses four and five: "He must be one who manages his own household well, keeping his children under control with all dignity (but if a man does not know how to manage his own household, how will he take care of the church of God?)." As a former school principal and owner of a manufacturing company, I know what the word "manage" means. A manager presides over and leads those he is responsible for. Christian husbands are the God-appointed managers of their homes. It is important that we fulfill our scriptural role by taking leadership in the home. Emilie began to respect me more when she saw in me the desire to be the manager of our home.

In his book *Christian Living in the Home,* Jay Adams gives an excellent explanation of the husband's role as the manager of the home:

> A good manager knows how to put other people to work...
> He will be careful not to neglect or destroy his wife's abilities.
> Rather, he will use them to the fullest...He does not consider
> her someone to be dragged along. Rather, he thinks of her as
> a useful, helpful and wonderful blessing from God...A man-
> ager has an eye focused on all that is happening in his house,
> but he does not do everything himself. Instead, he looks at
> the whole picture and keeps everything under control. He
> knows everything that is going on, how it is operating, and
> only when it is necessary to do so, steps in to change and to
> modify or in some way to help.[2]

During the 1950s when Emilie and I were married, husband and wife roles were much more clearly defined. In those days the husband took care of everything outside the house and the wife concerned herself with everything inside the house. We heard phrases like: "That's not my job." "I'm not changing the diapers—that's a mother's job." "The yard needs mowing—Dad and the boys will do it." Fortunately Emilie and I did not contract our marriage on that basis. I had seen my father do many jobs around the home that were considered "woman's work." So I had no problems helping with the dishes, changing diapers, babysitting while Emilie went to the market, ironing my own shirts, and even doing the laundry occasionally.

Also during the '50s, the man of the house was to write the checks and control the purse strings. We were warned that it was almost unchristian for the wife to pay the monthly bills. But I couldn't go along with it. I had a wife who was very good at finances. We established a budget together for our fixed expenses and decided together where to spend our money. Because Emilie was so good with numbers, I asked her to write the checks. This was difficult for her at first because she thought I needed to be responsible for our finances. But we figured it out together and it now works wonderfully.

Today the guidelines for management in the home have changed drastically. Gone are the days when the fathers went to work and earned the money while the mothers stayed home to take care of the children. The working mother is now a staple in the workforce. We recently met a retired man who stays home to cook delicious meals and keep house while his wife maintains a job outside the home. They love their new roles.

Not long ago Emilie and I ran into a former coworker of mine in a grocery store. I asked about his family, and he said that he quit his job to stay home and raise the children. His wife was so successful in her computer career and making so much more money than he could make, they had decided to reverse roles. He loved his duties at home and she loved her career much more than homemaking.

As these examples suggest, managing today's home and family is a responsibility that can be delegated in a number of ways. Each family is unique and free to decide what arrangement works best for them, even if it is different from any other family. The most important concern is that you weigh the variables unique to your family and establish a plan. As the biblical managers of our homes, we men are responsible to see that a plan is put into action. We may not always be right, and we may need to change the plan from time to time. But it is our responsibility to lead our families in establishing, evaluating, and modifying plans of action that effectively meet the needs of our wives and children.

The greatest enemy of the successful husband and manager is passivity. We tend to want to lay back and let things happen instead of step forward and make things happen in our homes. We cannot yield to the temptation to abandon our God-given role. We must get on with the program. When we do, our wives and our children will have greater respect for us.

The biblical pattern for the husband's role in managing the home is found in 1 Corinthians 11:3: "Now I want you to realize that the head of every man is Christ, and the head of every woman is man, and the head of Christ is God" (NIV). The chain of command is clear: God above Christ, Christ above man, man above woman. This principle is often difficult to maintain in our culture, but if we are to survive the attacks on the family today, we must return to God's manual on the subject and follow His plan. When you accept the role of a responsible manager and carry it out with the heart of a servant, your family will flourish.

I am so thankful that I had a mom who raised me with chores and responsibilities in the home. I've always been able to do domestic chores because of my early training. When Emilie and I got married, I loved helping her with food preparation, setting the table properly, clearing off the dirty dishes, loading the dishwasher, running a load of laundry, ironing if needed, and so forth.

Boy, I am glad I knew how to do all of these things when Emilie came down with cancer and had to have a bone marrow transplant in 2000. She wasn't able to do most of her domestic engineering responsibilities for four and a half years. If I hadn't learned all of the inside-the-home responsibilities, I would've been a cripple. But because I learned along the way how to function in the home, I was able to carry on our daily activities without having to hire someone to come in to assist me in caring for Emilie and our home.

A cute story came about through this experience. One of Emilie's lady friends from out of town would periodically come to spend a weekend with us to give me some relief. She observed that I knew how to do everything regarding keeping a home functioning. It made her think what her husband would do if she got sick for any length of time. She went home and shared how I was able to do everything in the home from menu planning to ironing the clothes. She asked her husband what he would do if she got sick. He thought for a moment and answered, "I would go live with Bob!"

All of us, if we live long enough, will have to be a caregiver for a sick wife. I know it's hard thinking about that when you are young, but believe me the golden years will come and they are not always golden.

Use this time as a training season of your life so that when that time comes (and it will) you will have the necessary tools and attitude to serve your wife.

Secrets to Romancing Your Marriage

- ⇛ Ask your wife if she has three or four specific needs you can work on meeting.
- ⇛ Call your wife and tell her you can't wait until you can come home to see her this evening.
- ⇛ Make an unexpected date with your wife for lunch during the middle of the day—your treat.
- ⇛ What about your mate sparks your romantic interest? Let her know.

9

The Oneness of Marriage

For this reason a man shall leave his father and
his mother, and be joined to his wife;
and they shall become one flesh. And the man
and his wife were both naked and were not ashamed.

GENESIS 2:24-25

God says that a husband and wife "shall become one flesh." In God's sight we become one at the altar when we share our vows of commitment. But practically speaking, oneness between a husband and wife is a process that happens over a period of time—your lifetime together.

It is very difficult to move from only caring for yourself to sharing your entire life with another person. And the older you are when you marry, the more difficult it becomes because you are more set in your ways. Emilie and I had very different backgrounds in family, religion, finances, tastes, and holiday celebrations. She came from the home of a verbally and physically abusive alcoholic father. I came from a warm, loving family where yelling and screaming were inappropriate. It took us only a few moments to enter into oneness by saying our vows. But we have spent the years of our marriage blending our different lives and building the oneness that we enjoy today.

Oneness doesn't mean sameness. Oneness refers to an agreement in commitment, mission in life, goals, and dreams. We sometimes teach seminars in Oceanside, California, near the marine base at Camp Pendleton. It is easy to identify marines in Oceanside even when they aren't in uniform. There is an external conformity about them—short haircuts, muscular bodies, straight backs, and a certain walk. But in marriage it is *internal* conformity that expresses oneness.

The picture of oneness in marriage is that of total unselfishness as we allow God to shape each partner. Oneness emerges as two different individuals reflect the same Christ. And spiritual oneness produces tremendous strength and unity in a family.

One of Aesop's tales illustrates the strength of this inner unity. A farmer had a very quarrelsome family. After vainly trying to reconcile his bickering sons, the farmer decided to teach them by example. He instructed his sons to bring him a bundle of sticks. After he tied the bundle securely, the farmer told each of his sons to try and break the bundle of sticks. They all tried and failed. Then the farmer untied the bundle and gave his sons the sticks to break one by one, which they did easily. The father said, "As long as you remain united, you are a match for your enemies. But separate and you are easily defeated."

To be one in marriage, a couple must be strong in the Lord. When we are one in Him, Satan cannot break us.

One of the great passages of Scripture is found in Ruth 1:16-17. When Ruth accompanies her mother-in-law, Naomi, on the journey back to Bethlehem, Ruth states this classic reply of oneness:

> Don't ask me to leave you and turn back. Wherever you go, I will go; wherever you live, I will live. Your people will be my people, and your God will be my God… May the LORD punish me severely if I allow anything but death to separate us! (NLT).

May this be your pledge as a couple: We stand together and we die together. That's the pledge we made with our marriage vows when we uttered, "For better or worse, in sickness and in health, for richer or for poorer, until death do us part."

You will never become one when each of you is going your separate way. There are new responsibilities when you say, "I do." Where certain activities were okay as a single person, they might not be so acceptable as a married couple. Oneness does not mean selfishness. It means just the opposite—it means humbleness. It means as a husband, I will put you above me. I will honor you as my wife. You are my number one priority after God. I have to take a look at my old single days and say, "There will be some changes made today." Does that mean you cut off all your old friends and activities? Absolutely not, but it does mean you have to consider your wife when those friends and activities are eating into your oneness with your wife.

Wives, you also have the obligation to evaluate your old single friends and activities. Some of these you may have to say "no" to and realize they aren't as important as having a husband who you need to honor with your time, energy, and attention. The "oneness factor" means you both will learn to "say 'no' to good things and save your 'yeses' for the best."

Each day as you start a new day declare that you choose to become one with your mate. Love is a choice.

Sexuality

Genesis tells us that Adam and Eve "were both naked and were not ashamed." That was the age of innocence. But today we live in a society that is cluttered with the debris of fallen man. Broken relationships are everywhere. As I watch the television talk shows and hear the rich, the famous, the sex therapists, and the various movement leaders express their views on marriage, I pray that God will protect the hearers from all the garbage pouring out of these "experts." The only true expert on marriage is God, the One who designed it. And His manual on marriage is the Bible.

Before sin entered the world in the Garden of Eden, Adam and Eve lived naked and unashamed. The Hebrew word for "naked" simply means laid bare. Adam and Eve were completely open and transparent with each other—no hang-ups or embarrassments. Because they hid nothing from one another, they had nothing to be ashamed about.

It is no accident that this kind of openness in sexuality comes after departure, permanence, and oneness. When we give priority to the first three, we will experience the fullness of sexuality as God designed it. Often we want sexuality to be first while we work on the other three, but that's not God's order. For example, we men have little difficulty becoming sexually stimulated and performing intercourse very quickly. But our wives are different, and they don't respond quite as quickly. The setting must be just right, with no disturbances, and they need to be in a loving frame of mind. A wife will respond to sexual intimacy better if she knows that her man has made his break with his family and made her his top priority (departure), that he is totally committed to her (permanence), and that they share the same goals and dreams (oneness).

Sexual Differences

Our society fosters cultural differences between men and women. God Himself, though, created us physically different, psychologically different, and sexually different. Bob and I came into marriage with very different attitudes toward sex. Bob thought, *Wow!* But my mom didn't share with me too much enthusiasm. She thought sex was the *duty* of the wife and was not to be enjoyed. Bob soon learned that our difference was a big issue. Fortunately for me, I was married to a very tender and considerate young man. Both men and women need to be aware of the differences, or we will never have our sexual needs met.

Most women are first attracted to a man, and then they move to feelings of love. Wanting to be sexual with her man comes later, when she can trust him (hopefully for both it will occur on their wedding night).

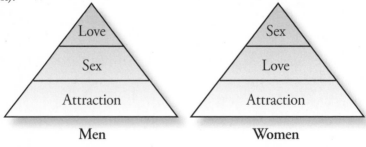

Bob quickly realized that what I desired most in marriage was love, not sex. I desired sexual fulfillment, yes, but I viewed sex as a by-product of love. Where you, as a man, grow in your love for your wife through sexual fulfillment, a woman finds sexual fulfillment when she is sure of her husband's love. When Bob realized I placed more value on love, affection, and romance, he had to slow down and make sure that our sex came out of *agape* love rather than just *eros* love. Do you need to slow down? If you love your wife in a nonsexual way first, you will find that both of you will achieve sexual fulfillment.

Other ways that women differ from men when it comes to sexuality:

- Women love to be romanced with flowers, a love note, a box of candy, or suggestions of intimacy.
- They like to be talked to while making love—to be told how you are feeling, what you want, and how you appreciate them. Conversation builds intimacy and excitement for them.
- They like to take their time when being loved. They take longer than you to become fully aroused sexually.
- They need to feel emotionally secure to become fully aroused sexually.
- They want you to respect your body and hers.
- They need patient and gentle attention as well as verbal appreciation.

What have you learned about your wife from this discussion of sexual differences? How can you stand by her and support her despite the ways she differs from you sexually? The longer you are married, the more you will see that happiness in marriage doesn't just happen. Hold hands with your wife and tell her of your love. Don't take her for granted. Love with a willing heart.

The key to a fulfilling sex life is openness and transparency between husband and wife. In a later chapter on communication, we will deal more completely with the topic of transparency between two partners.

Secrets to Romancing Your Marriage

- ≋ Cut down on the amount of TV you watch every day.
- ≋ Rest and relax. Recline and read.
- ≋ Let go of external measures of your sense of self and worth.
- ≋ Write out what your priorities are for the month. Be sure to block out time for each other.
- ≋ Show your real emotions today.
- ≋ Consider eliminating things that aren't that gratifying to you or to your spouse.
- ≋ Be vulnerable and honest with your spouse.
- ≋ Celebrate your oneness with a romantic evening.

10

Making a Great Marriage

*A happy marriage is the union
of two good forgivers.*
–Robert Quillen

Because Bob and I now have gray hair and have been together so long, young couples are always asking us, "What makes a great marriage?" At this stage in life, I can be very direct in my response: "God's Word has been the foundation for Bob and me. Our secret equation is: God's prescription + our committed efforts = marital fullness."

As we have worked to apply God's teachings to our marriage, we have discovered five principles for growing a great marriage. We use the following "GREAT" acrostic to relate these principles to others:

G—Giving

R—Relating

E—Edifying

A—Allowing your mate to be God's person

T—Touching

Giving

God's nature is to give, and He is continually giving His free gifts to us. His plan for us is to be continual givers also. In marriage that means we must give to one another our time, our talents, our hearts, ourselves, our love, our finances, our gifts, our thoughts, our trust, and our fears.

When Bob and I stopped thinking about ourselves and started giving to each other, our relationship improved. Some of the little gifts we have given each other that have received positive responses are notes sent through the mail, a card of love tucked in a purse or lunch sack, words of encouragement, a bouquet of flowers, a new book to discuss, time in the evening for conversation, minivacations together, and a dinner out at least twice a month.

We also found that when we started giving to each other, it became easier for us to give to others. The circle of giving soon spread to people we didn't even know.

Relating

Relating to another person means that you connect with them, you understand them, and you "get" what they are about. If any two

Getters generally don't get happiness;
givers get it. You simply give to others a bit of your-
self—a thoughtful act, a helpful idea,
a word of appreciation, a lift over a rough spot, a
sense of understanding, a timely suggestion.
You take something out of your mind, garnished in
kindness out of your heart, and put it into the other
fellow's mind and heart.

—CHARLES H. BURR

people must connect in thought and meaning, it is husband and wife! Relating is a primary avenue to oneness in marriage. This can only happen when partners spend much time together talking, listening, and learning what makes each other tick and ticked. This is very difficult for people who don't express themselves well. I was very hesitant to speak during Bob's and my early courtship because I feared I would say the wrong thing and blow our relationship. With Bob's encouragement, I overcame my shyness. Now I have no trouble expressing myself. I give my Bob much of the credit for improving my ability to relate not only with him, but with others.

A passage of Scripture we often use when teaching couples how to relate is Proverbs 24:3-4: "By wisdom a house is built, and by understanding it is established; and by knowledge the rooms are filled with all precious and pleasant riches." There are three key words that stand out in these two verses:

- wisdom
- understanding
- knowledge

We gain these three qualities by studying the Scriptures, reading relevant books, and attending workshops and seminars. We can't learn these three strengths by doing nothing. We have to be active in acquiring them.

In marriage we are to study our mates thoroughly in order to gain wisdom, understanding, and knowledge about them. How do we study them? By relating to them through open, genuine conversation.

One man I heard about lost $250,000 through the stock market. How would you react if you watched a quarter of a million dollars disappear before your very eyes? Would you jump off a bridge or get drunk? Fortunately this man had learned that his home was a "trauma center." He phoned his wife and calmly told her what had happened. Then he asked her for a date that evening. They went out to dinner and discussed the day's happening together, just like they had done many

> *The only basis for real fellowship with God and man is to live out in the open with both.*
>
> –ROY HESSION

times before with far less shattering events. Thank the Lord this couple had learned to relate!

Relating doesn't happen automatically. Growing in communication takes a lot of hard, well-planned work. Marital wisdom, understanding, and knowledge come through many patient hours of relating. But there is a reward for our labors. The "precious and pleasant riches" we gain from our efforts are positive attitudes, good relationships, pleasant memories, mutual respect, and depth of character.

Edifying

One way a wife feels loved is when her husband and children lift her up with praise. Women (actually everyone!) just love to hear words that build them up. Words and phrases such as...

- "Mom, this was a really good breakfast."
- "Thanks for supporting me at school."
- "You are a really great mom and wife."
- "You make me feel like a king when I come home."
- "I really appreciate how you make our house a home."

Communication is a major channel by which we edify one another. If our goal is to lift someone up, we make a choice to be positive in our words and action while around each other. We realize that positive words build up and heal, while negative words destroy and tear down.

One way to check our attitude is to constantly ask, "Is this edifying?" If not, shape up and go positive. Each person would do well to keep that question in the forefront of his mind to make sure the conversation stays encouraging.

> It takes so little to make us sad,
> Just a sighting word or doubting sneer,
> Just a scornful smile on some lips held dear;
> And our footsteps lag, though the goal seemed near,
> And we lose our courage and hope we had—
> So little it takes to make us sad.
>
> It takes so little to make us glad,
> Just a cheering clasp of a friendly hand,
> Just a word from one who can understand;
> And we finish the task we long had planned,
> And we lose the doubt and the fear we had—
> So little it takes to make us glad.
>
> –IDA GOLDSMITH MORRIS

Allowing Your Mate to Be God's Person

One of the hardest lessons about trusting God in our marriages is allowing Him to be the change agent in our mates. Far too often we think we are ordained by God to change them. One way to deal with the urge to change our mates is to concentrate on the positives and let God deal with the negatives. You might use a chart like the following one to help you and your mate identify areas that you would like to improve in your lives with the help of the Holy Spirit. Remember, although you can mention areas you'd like your mate to think about, the change is up to them and God. Don't nag. And you also must be open to your mate's suggested changes.

Bob and I have always wanted the best for each other. One of our goals has been to avoid competition between us. We are to complement each other. If one of us gets lifted up in some fashion, the other says, "Thank You, God, for blessing Bob/Emilie."

When Bob was in education, I was always known as Bob's wife. But for the last several years, since God has blessed my writing and speaking ministry, Bob has been known as my husband. This reversal initially was a threat to him, even though he was excited for me. Bob had always been the main provider, and he loved the spotlight. Suddenly he was playing second fiddle behind me. He had to ask himself if he wanted to glorify himself or did he want to bring glory to God through my ministry. Every time the question was asked, the same answer came back—glorify God. It took some time for Bob to realize that he felt comfortable with this change in our lives. He can honestly say now that as long as Jesus is lifted up in *our* ministry, he will serve in whatever capacity Jesus wants to use him.

It's so easy to get caught up in the world's mind-set of being in competition with everyone—including your mate. Satan would love to divide your strengths, talents, and gifts by seeing you work against each other. He will prey on your insecurities and drive a wedge between you and your spouse, fracturing your unity.

Category of Expectation	Strengths	Desired Change	Action for Change
Personal habits	very neat picks up clothes hangs towels puts away shoes	shower daily shampoo hair regularly	talk to him about these areas let God work in this area
Children	_____	_____	_____
Finances	_____	_____	_____
Sex	_____	_____	_____
Spiritual	_____	_____	_____
Social	_____	_____	_____
Aspirations	_____	_____	_____
Time	_____	_____	_____

Become encouragers for one another. Be excited about your mate's successes. Be there to comfort your partner when the contract isn't signed, the deal falls through, sickness slows her down, the license isn't renewed, and so forth. If you learn to submit to each other by the power of the Holy Spirit, you can allow each other to be God's worker.

Touching

Can you remember when a parent, teacher, or coach wrapped his or her arm around you or patted you gently to indicate that everything was going to be okay? A loving touch has healing power and communicates that we are accepted. If children live with touching parents, they too will learn to touch people in healthy ways. We say around our home that everybody needs at least one hug a day to stay healthy.

Touching is also an important element in establishing a good marriage. Bob and I have found nonsexual touching to be an excellent way to transmit helpful encouragement to each other. Some of us come from very affectionate families, some do not. It's hard for non-touchers to become touchers, but with prayer and patience, even the most reserved person can become open to affectionate, loving touch.

Men, most women like a hug, an arm around the shoulders, holding hands in a movie, a gentle neck rub. She perceives your touch as saying, "I love you." And touching doesn't always have to lead to the bedroom, which many times is the man's goal. However, don't always rule out that objective.

> *Give your wife a shoulder rub after her evening bath or shower. Tell her before you start that you don't want one in return. Let her truly relax and enjoy the experience.*

> *Remember, the choices you make today will determine the kind of marriage you will have in the years to come so choose wisely. Choose love for a lifetime.*
>
> —RICHARD EXLEY

Affectionate touching between Mom and Dad also sends signals to the children that their parents love each other. Children are comforted by the security of knowing their parents are lovingly committed to each other.

These five elements of a great marriage don't just happen. And the mere presence of these elements doesn't guarantee the success of a marriage, but they certainly hold the potential to enrich an already strong marriage or energize a slumping one.

The following lines are worth reading, rereading, and pondering. They communicate volumes about great marriages.

- All marriages aren't happy—living together is tough.
- A good marriage is not a gift—it's an achievement by God's grace.
- Marriage is not for children—it takes guts and maturity.
- Marriage separates the men from the boys and the women from the girls.
- Marriage is tested daily by the ability to compromise.
- The survival of marriage can depend on being smart enough to know what's worth fighting about, making an issue of, or even mentioning.
- Marriage is giving and, more importantly, forgiving.
- With all its ups and downs, marriage is still God's best object lesson of Jesus and the church.

- Through submission to one another, we can witness to the world that marriage does work and is still alive.

Secrets to Romancing Your Marriage

⇝ Put the work and love into your marriage now.

⇝ Devote time to each of the "GREAT" principles.

⇝ Hold hands more often. You'll find yourself feeling more connected to one another.

⇝ Recognize the gifts and abilities of your spouse and encourage those strengths.

⇝ Pray about your strengths, so that you can become who God wants you to be.

⇝ Stop trying to change your spouse...leave that to the Holy Spirit.

⇝ Find new ways to relate to your spouse. Share in activities and goals and conversations!

Growing Together Despite Differences

They are no longer two, but one flesh.
What therefore God has joined together,
let no man separate.

MATTHEW 19:6

How do we become one when we are so different? This is such an exciting journey! Bob and I had the same question put before us as we established our first home (a rented apartment). We were so different:

Emilie	Bob
Jewish	Baptist
high school graduate	master's degree
lived in an apartment	lived in 3-bedroom home
didn't know Jesus	believed in Jesus as Savior
father had passed away	mother and father were at home
working mom	stay-at-home mom
rode city buses	owned a car
never had a Christmas tree	always had a Christmas tree
loved fruits and steamed vegetables	loved meat, potatoes, and gravy
17 years old	22 years old
still in high school	started first year teaching

nonathletic	athletic
organized	not organized
never had an animal	had dogs, cats, and horses
born in the city	born on a farm

Needless to say, we were told, "It'll never work! You have too many differences that will prevent you two from becoming *one*." But our faith said we could. I'm so glad we listened to Scripture rather than the words of the disbelievers because we've enjoyed many years together and the joy of our two children (Brad and Jenny) and five grandchildren (Christine, Chad, Bevan, Bradley Joe, and Weston).

If we can do it, so can you! This chapter deals specifically with taking two individuals with differing backgrounds and making them one in the sight of God.

As Bob and I encounter many women attending our seminars or seeking counseling who are plagued by disquieting concerns and questions about their relations with their mates, we hear comments like these all the time:

- "My husband says he's tired of talking at work and just wants to relax when he comes home. Why won't he talk to me?"

- "My husband doesn't spend any time with the children, and he expects me to handle all the discipline. How can I get him to take some responsibility?"

- "My husband blames me for a messy house, but he won't clean up his mess. Are all husbands this sloppy?"

- "My husband works late at the office and golfs on Saturdays. We never see him at home. Why doesn't he enjoy family life as I do?"

- "My husband never makes a decision; he wants me to decide. He says his job is all he wants to think about."

- "My husband is always depressed. What can I do about it?"

- "Why do I get the feeling that my husband wants me to be his mother instead of his wife?"

- "My husband is rarely romantic and never shows his emotions. Why?"

- "My husband tells our sons to be tough and to fight for their rights. I disagree with him, but he says that's the way boys should be."

Similarly, a lot of men catch our ear with their complaints about their wives:

- "I don't mind talking when I get home from work, but for two hours?"

- "My wife has spoiled the children all these years, and now she wants me to discipline them."

- "My wife has nothing to do all day but take care of the house, but it's always a mess when I come home. What's she doing all day?"

- "I try not to go home early after work or be home during weekends. With the wife and kids home, there's nothing but confusion—loud voices, doors slamming, and everything lying around in a mess."

- "I won't decide where the family is to go on an outing anymore because when I do, nobody wants to go there."

- "My only source of depression is that I don't make enough money or have a prestigious job title that meets my wife's approval."

- "My wife wants me to be romantic and huggy all the time. But I can't waste my time doing that when I've got so many other things to do."

- "My wife wants to make sissies out of our boys. She wants them to take piano and dance lessons, but I want them to be football players."

> *It is God's will*
> *in every marriage*
> *that the couple*
> *love each other*
> *with an absorbing,*
> *spiritual, emotional,*
> *and physical*
> *attraction that*
> *continues to grow*
> *throughout their*
> *lifetime together.*
>
> –ED WHEAT

Marital friction does not come from husbands and wives being physically, emotionally, psychologically, and culturally different as much as it comes from not *understanding* the differences and accommodating them in their relationships.

Although the world, with its unisex fashions and equal rights movements, loudly argues that there are no differences between the sexes, those of us who are married know otherwise. What circumstances have caused you to realize just how differently you and your spouse think? What situations have brought to the foreground the differences between how you each act?

What can a good husband do in the face of these differences? He can acknowledge and accept how his wife is different from him. Such acceptance comes more easily when we remember that God made man and woman different. We also need to be aware that some of the differences are due to our individual characteristics. You entered into marriage with certain strengths and certain weaknesses. I encourage you not to be threatened by differences between you and your loved one, but discover how these differences make the relationship stronger.

Why Differences Matter

The most obvious differences between men and women are physical. But that is not frequently the cause of trouble in a marriage. It is when we don't understand the psychological differences that we encounter more arguments, divisions, and frustrations. We approach tasks, relationships, love, and life differently.

Doreen Kimura elaborates on the differences between the male and female brain in an article in *Psychology Today:*

> Sexual differences in the way the brain is organized suggest different ways of thinking and learning. The male brain is specialized. He uses one side for solving spatial problems, the other side for defining a word or verbalizing a problem. The female brain is not so specialized for some functions such as defining words. A woman's right brain and left brain abilities are duplicated to some extent in each hemisphere and work together to solve problems.[1]

Women can shift from right brain to left brain activities very quickly, and many times they rely on both hemispheres at the same time. Not men! You have to come to a screeching halt in the left brain before you shift to the right brain. There is nothing wrong with men. That's how God created their brains to work!

This data on right brain and left brain explains several psychological differences between men and women.

- Women can better sense the difference between what people say and what they mean.
- Men have difficulty understanding women's intuition, often thinking that women are too sensitive.
- Women are more perceptive about people and the meaning of feelings than men are.
- Men and women approach problem solving differently. Men are more analytical and deal with the problem more objectively. Women are less objective; they personally identify with the problem.
- Women can work on several projects at once. Men want to concentrate on only one thing at a time.[2]

Dr. Daniel G. Amen in his book *Healing the Hardware of the Soul* makes several observations regarding men and women:

> When we are bonded to people in a positive way, we feel better about our lives and ourselves. The deep limbic system of the brain tends to be larger in women. This may account for the reality that women in overwhelming numbers are the primary caretakers for children and the elderly. The larger limbic system size seems to make emotional connections easier for women. Women tend to have more friends; they go to church, and they pray—what I call bonding with God— more than men. Women have a stronger nesting instinct than men, which appears to reflect a great biological need to have their houses in order.[3]

Cultural Differences

The physical and psychological differences between men and women give rise to several cultural differences, although it is some- times difficult to determine where the unlearned hormonal differences leave off and the learned cultural differences begin. Let's take a look at marriage, commitment, and success in the business world.

In *Why Men Are the Way They Are,* author Warren Farrell states that men are performers who feel they must have an acceptable level of production to be fulfilled. As a performer, a man is competitive and goal-oriented. As an initiator, he is vulnerable to risk and failure and, as a result, often defensive in his relationships—even with his wife.

Long-term relationships are risky for a man because they expose his weaknesses, making him vulnerable to hurt and possible defeat. Instead of moving closer to his woman, a man will defend himself from hurt and defeat by escaping the relationship. If he doesn't stay, his wife cannot hurt him or prove him to be a failure. (Statistics show that men are more apt to leave their marriages than women.) To compensate, if not to ensure against failure in his relationships, a man works hard to succeed in business. After all, he rationalizes, if he is successful in the working world, he can buy whatever he needs to raise his sense of identity to a level he can live with, even if he is not successful on the home front. Success at work protects many men from the pain of their failure at home.[4]

A man's failure in business often produces characteristics that make him unlovable at home. When Bob was working on his master's degree, he was not always pleasant to live with. I thought he should value the things I valued (such as home life and child rearing), but he was busy—perhaps too busy at times—making his mark on the world. I didn't always understand his desire for success and approval on the job.

Our culture encourages this drive for success and holds up many other standards for "real" men to achieve. Which of the following ideas from today's culture are seeds of conflict in your marriage?

- The man is to be the breadwinner in the family. If his wife works, he feels he is less than a "real" man.
- Men don't quit until they are carried off the field.
- Being macho is important. A man must be in shape, drive the right car, and belong to the right clubs.
- Men must know about "men things"—boats, trucks, planes, cars, sports, and so on.
- Men always read masculine magazines and never look at women's magazines.
- A man can perform sexually under any circumstances, on demand, and repeatedly.

These ideas seem based on learned cultural differences rather than hormonal differences, but it's not always easy to determine which is which. When a man comes home after a busy day, he has already accomplished what he feels is really important: He has won the battles at the shop, office, or store and provided for his family. He wants to relax, watch television, and read the paper. His wife, however, has waited all day for him and is excited that he is home. He's ready to kick back, but she's ready to kick into gear. She wants to talk.

Tasks vs. Relationships

In her book *In a Different World,* Carol Gilligan summarizes the tension caused by the male's orientation toward tasks and the female's orientation toward relationships:

> Since masculinity is defined through separation while femininity is defined through attachment, male gender identity is threatened by intimacy while female gender identity is threatened by separation. Thus, males tend to have difficulty with relationships while females tend to have difficulty with individualization.[5]

In the academic world, the question again arises: How much of this task-orientation versus relationship-orientation is due to hormonal differences and how much is due to learned cultural differences? The article "Sexism in Our Schools—Training Girls for Failure" by Mary Conroy raises this question. What do the following statistics say to you?

- Girls start school with higher test scores than boys. By the time they take the SAT as juniors in high school, girls trail boys by 57 points.

- In coed colleges, women speak up in class 2.5 times less often than their male classmates.

- After the first year of college, women show sharper drops in self-confidence than men do. The longer women stay in school, the lower their self-confidence falls.

- Women receive fewer than 17 percent of all the doctorates awarded in math and physics.

- A mere 10 percent of all high-school principals are women—a smaller percentage than in the 1950s.

- Only 11 percent of all full professors are women.

In her article, Conroy presents data showing that teachers interact more with boys at every grade level—and it doesn't matter whether the teacher is male or female. The classroom scales tilt firmly in favor of boys, but not because teachers deliberately exclude girls. Most teachers aren't even aware that they treat boys and girls differently,

Yes, there are cultural differences in our schools, and these differences create tension between the sexes at a very early age.

Besides the primary cultural differences of task- and relationship-orientation, several other cultural differences between men and women—often framed from childhood—shape our role expectations in marriage:

- Blue is masculine and pink is feminine.

- Boys are supposed to be big, tough, and active, while girls are tiny, sweet, and passive.

- Boys should play with trucks, guns, and trains, while girls should choose dolls.

- Mothers are more affectionate with girls than boys. Boys are fussier than girls, and girls sleep better than boys.

- Boys are trained to be independent, and girls are trained to be compliant.

- Boys are competitive, and girls are cooperative.

- Boys form small groups and gangs. Girls develop one-on-one relationships.

- Boys play softball and tell war stories in the locker room. Girls have tea parties and share personal, intimate conversation.

- Girls pattern themselves after their mothers, but boys don't want to copy feminine traits because they fear they will look like sissies around boys.[6]

Where do you see differences between the male culture and female culture causing tension in your marriage? How can understanding the source of some of the differences between you and your wife help minimize the stress they cause?

We find ourselves in a transition period in our culture regarding the roles of men and women. Our Western culture is still very masculine in nature and emphasis. Our boys and men are taught to be tough, yet more and more they are encouraged to be tender. They learn early to take risks and take control, but their wives urge them to be vulnerable and transparent. Men generally feel more secure in mirroring traditional roles, but they are finding that today's woman needs a sensitive, caring man more than a Mr. Macho.

As men become more firmly established in the traditional male roles, they become more hostile in rejecting the female role.

Secrets to Understanding

Men and women, as different as we are from one another, are made in God's image (Genesis 1:27), and God called this creation good. A Christian husband and wife can be confident that God put males and females on the earth for a special purpose. To help us bridge our God-given differences, Jesus offers us fundamental guidelines for how to respond to each other. In Matthew 22:37-39, He simply and directly states the greatest commandments in the Scriptures: "You shall love the Lord your God with all your heart, and with all your soul, and with all your mind" and "You shall love your neighbor as yourself."

First, you are to love God, and part of loving God is honoring His creation. Accept what God has made—unique men and women created for a special purpose. Second, you are to love others, particularly the mate God has given you. Loving your wife doesn't mean changing her. That's the Holy Spirit's job. Loving your wife means understanding how she is different from you and accepting her as she is. I think that one of the lessons of Proverbs 24:3—"By wisdom a house is built, and through understanding it is established" (NIV)—is that a loving understanding for each other as husband and wife solidly establishes your marriage and your family. Continuously seeking to understand leads to less anger and frustration. You may still become irritated, frustrated, and disturbed by some of your mate's actions, but at least you will be growing in your knowledge of why she is doing what she is doing.

In Romans 12:2, the apostle Paul offers another scriptural guideline for dealing with differences in our marriages. "Do not be conformed to this world, but be transformed by the renewing of your mind, so that you may prove what the will of God is, that which is good and acceptable and perfect." Our culture teaches us to stand up for our individuality and our rights. We're not encouraged to give into or accommodate another person's different views.

But Paul directs us not to conform to that standard, but to be transformed by the renewing of our minds. We are to let God's teaching on the blending of differences permeate our thinking and, subsequently, our acting. The rewards of this are positive attitudes, good relationships, pleasant memories, mutual respect, and depth of character. We have a choice. We can live in a war zone fueled by our differences as men and women. Or we can live in a house filled with the precious and pleasant riches which come from understanding and accepting our differences.

Perhaps the greatest enemy of understanding and accepting differences is pride. God hates pride, yet we seem to struggle against it in everything we do, especially us men. We must break down the walls of pride, which our differences erect, to enjoy the rewards that understanding promises.

Our Creator God has created us distinct and very different from one another. When we accept those differences as God-given and even blessed by Him, we will experience the rewards of more positive attitudes, better relationships, mutual respect, and godly character.

Delightfully Different

Bob and I have experienced the entire gamut of differences discussed in this chapter. We have learned to see ourselves as delightfully different from one another. Despite different backgrounds and all the physical, emotional, and cultural differences, there isn't an air of competition between us. We want to complement each other. We are committed to Christ as the foundation of our home and our relationship. Bob is committed to loving me as Christ loves the church, and I am dedicated to being his helpmate, respecting him as my husband (Ephesians 5:25,31). These points of agreement enable us to work around differences in positive ways.

> *The most difficult years of marriage are those following the wedding.*

After studying Scripture, Bob and I realized that we were both made for the purpose of worshiping and enjoying God, that we had each been wonderfully created with unique male or female characteristics, and that we were, with God's blessing, to complement one another according to His plan. God's Word helped us see marriage afresh and to understand His design for this institution. Every question we had regarding our differences was answered by Scripture. We simply needed to study and apply the truth to our lives. As each of us came closer to God through studying His Word, we came to know each other better too. Gradually our differences and inadequacies became less effective instruments in Satan's hands to weaken our marriage and neutralize our ministry.

Secrets to Romancing Your Marriage

- ≫ Men, be in complete charge of your children for a morning or an afternoon. Tell your wife she is free to stay home or go out.
- ≫ Men, learn to delegate more at work. Come home at a reasonable hour to spend with your wife and family.

≫ Both husband and wife try being totally positive, accepting, supportive, and nonjudgmental for one entire week. No complaining, nagging, or preaching.

≫ Take a risk—be romantic.

≫ Rent a convertible on a sunny day and cruise around—just the two of you.

≫ Serve your spouse breakfast on Saturday morning.

≫ While on the road, send your spouse a postcard every day you're away.

≫ Write your spouse a love letter and mail it to your home.

≫ Record your favorite love songs from the time you were dating and play them in the car as you travel.

Meeting Your Wife's Needs

Be renewed in the spirit of your mind, and put
on the new self, which in the likeness of God
has been created in righteousness and holiness of the truth.

EPHESIANS 4:23-24

In *His Needs, Her Needs,* author Willard Harley Jr. has listed five basic needs that a wife brings to a marriage: affection, conversation, honesty and openness, financial support, and family commitment.[1]

Recognizing and meeting these needs for her will mean a stronger marriage and the ability to get through the rocky times that happen in all marriages. A wife benefits greatly when her husband recognizes her needs and does his best to meet them—without always having to be asked. Men, we have to anticipate, we have to think, we have to get with the program—whatever that might be.

Your wife feels loved when you are willing to help her out. Don't wait to be asked if you can help—just help. Then look her in the eye and say, "Just another way to say I love you!"

Scripture teaches the importance of helping when needed. The writer of Ecclesiastes notes that "two are better than one because they have a good return for their labor. For if either of them falls, the one will lift up his companion. But woe to the one who falls when there is not another to lift him up" (4:9-10). In Galatians 6:2, Paul calls believers to "bear one another's burdens, and thereby fulfill the law of Christ." Again and again, Scripture reminds us of the importance of helping when times are difficult. Reaching out to help and accepting help gets our needs met and creates a special bond with the person we allow near.

A wife feels loved when you, her husband, trust her with your emotions. It is not a sign of weakness for a husband to share with his wife this way.

Affection

Women don't approach love the same way men do. Men are driven by their *eros* drive and can move into sexual desire even before love appears. Bob thought I would feel like him when it came to intimacy. What I desired in marriage was love—not sex. Men perceive they are loved when they have sex with their wives, whereas women love first and then think about sex. You as a man grow in your love for your wife through sexual fulfillment, whereas your wife finds greater sexual fulfillment when she is assured of her husband's love.

Men can usually function sexually on the basis of eroticism and physical stimulation alone. A man can become aroused at a selfish level with any woman who is available. It is easy for a man to engage in sex outside of love. Women, on the other hand, generally are more emotionally oriented. Though they are capable of being intensely erotic, a woman usually responds sexually to a man who provides security, understanding, tenderness, and compassion. Women who have extramarital affairs usually do so because they are angry, lonely, insecure, or generally unfulfilled in their marriage relationship.

When wives are lonely or unfulfilled because their husbands don't spend time with them, they will be less likely to respond in a positive way to sexual advances. Dr. Kevin Leman's book *Sex Begins in the Kitchen* captures this idea. He warns that men should not wait until bedtime to start getting romantic. He suggests you start setting the stage at breakfast with kind words and loving touches.[2] Leave a thoughtful note, give your wife a call during the day, give her a hug, a kiss, a wink, and a listening ear when you get home. She needs more than your sexual prowess to fulfill her. She needs all of you!

A primary way to develop intimacy and affection is through language. Women respond to words of encouragement, edifying words, words that build up. Bob and I express our love by using positive words:

- Thank you
- Please
- May I
- Yes
- I want to
- I would like
- I feel
- I will

You can never tell a woman enough times that you love her. Someone once asked Billy Graham how he and Ruth showed affection to each other. He replied, "We romance with our eyes." That might be hard to believe if you are a young man with a lot of sexual drive, but as you get older, you will begin to appreciate the deeper side of intimacy and affection. Let me tell you, it's a lot sweeter than just *eros* sex. In order to arrive at that stage in life, you have to communicate with each other in an endearing way—it takes years to understand.

Many times your wife just appreciates a hug, a touch, a pinch. These signs of affection don't always have to end up in the bedroom—it may, but it doesn't have to. A wife just wants to know that you care about her.

Conversation

Men, you have probably realized that your wife has a real need to talk. With the advent of cell phones, they talk more than ever. That's the part of being a woman a man can never understand. Women love to bond and are very relational. Men usually want to get to the bottom line and they will fill in the spaces. Some marriage experts say that the drive for women to talk is as strong as the drive for sex among men.

We know that this comparison is true. So, men, if you are attempting to understand what makes your wife different from you—it is her need to converse. Most women still have a lot more to say when hubby comes home from work and just wants peace and quiet. Husbands, be aware that she has been busy all day and has thought up a long list of items and topics to pass by your brain.

A wise man will be very patient in this area. If you don't express interest in what she wants to share, she eventually will find someone who will. Unfortunately in today's culture it might be another man.

Whenever Bob and I are communicating with God regularly through prayer and the study of His Word, we enjoy excellent dialog with each other. The closer Bob and I get to God, the closer we grow together as a couple. The inverse principle is also true: The farther we move away from God by not communicating with Him, the farther apart Bob and I become.

Honesty and Openness

According to Willard Harley, a woman's third need is honesty and openness. This need is so basic, yet many men struggle with the openness part. Why does this rate in the big five needs of your wife? Is it really that important? *Yes!*

One of the great marriage verses of Scripture is found in Genesis 2:24, which reads: "A man shall leave his father and his mother, and be joined to his wife; and they shall become one flesh." This is God's command to you as men. With your obedience to that command, you, as a believer, receive a blessing. The blessing is found in verse 25: "The man and his wife were both naked and were not ashamed." What this blessing promises is that if a man leaves his mother and father, joins to his wife, making themselves one, they will be transparent and open in their relationship. If the man shows commitment to his wife, they both can open up and not hide any secrets.

When the wife can trust her husband and know that they are both on the same page, she can open up and give her husband her affection unrestrainedly. Bob often tells men that if they want a great sex life, all they have to do is meet the three hurdles in these two verses and they too will receive the blessing of standing together naked and not being ashamed.

When there is this kind of openness, partners can give their spouses the truth. We don't have to be suspicious of any question that our mates might ask. This transparency allows honest communication. Whatever your mate asks you, you can be honest. Your spouse has a right to your innermost thoughts. As a couple you get to know each other better than any other person knows you or your wife. When a person knows you, they know the good and the bad. That's what it means to become "one."

Women usually find it easier to be open than men. Men can work toward becoming "tough and tender." I have found that when wives give their husbands a vote of confidence and don't always have a hidden agenda, the men feel more freedom to share their thoughts, dreams, and feelings. You men tend to be more cautious and hold back important parts of your lives until you feel safe.

Here's an important truth: Your wife will be more willing to go along with your dreams, plans, and thoughts if she can depend on and trust you because you are open and honest and loving. When you can honestly communicate with your wife, she has security and confidence in your future plans.

A wife's emotional stability is strengthened when she can trust her husband's words. As a man of good character, your wife will become secure. A secure wife is free to love...and express that love. Present yourself to your wife as you really are. That way she will better understand who you are and what you say.

It's Okay to Disagree

For many years I thought a couple was never to disagree—that Bob and I should agree at all times. Then I began to realize that this wasn't always possible because Bob and I came from different backgrounds. We can justify why we think a certain way because of the way we were raised. The problem with this is we both can support our respective choices. People tend to believe that the others in their lives should think like they do. But if this isn't true in real life, how can a couple always agree? Also, as I studied the basic temperament types, I soon realized that my Bob had a different temperament than I. We tend to respond differently to situations and ideas.

> *Love is not all that simple, it is an art that must be learned. We all can learn to love.*
>
> –AUTHOR UNKNOWN

With this new data, Bob and I gave each other permission to disagree. We became better listeners and weren't so defensive and argumentative. With our new knowledge, we weren't as easily frustrated when we didn't think alike. It was okay. We agreed to be able to disagree. What a freeing experience! With this in place, we were able to respect each other's diversity in opinions more. I had a more loving attitude toward Bob because he looked at me in a different way. My ideas and concerns were more important.

Because of this arrangement, Bob and I are much more able to be united in one mind, one love, one spirit, and one purpose. To this day we are strongly committed to the real issues of life. In the big issues we are as one; in the lesser issues we still differ—and that's what makes marriage so much fun.

Financial Support

One area of a woman's security need is that she marry a man who can and will support her and future children financially. This is not to say that women are gold diggers, but in the back of many of their minds they think, *Does this man I'm dating have the work ethic that will give me a secure feeling financially?*

A husband's inability to provide for the basic needs of a wife and children can cause real marital strain. Each woman comes into a relationship with differing expectations about what that economic level is, depending on what her childhood experiences were. Unfortunately many couples set a standard of living far higher than they are able to maintain on a husband's single salary.

A couple must decide if the wife is to be a homemaker, a career woman, or a combination of the two. I've found that today's woman feels she must work outside the home if she is going to have any significance in life. My belief is that a wife should be a homemaker during her children's growing-up years. Children need Mom to be home during their formative years. After they grow and leave home, the mom can have her career. There are many years left after she becomes an "empty nester."

> *Happy is the couple who tries to live on what they need, not on what they want.*
>
> –WILLARD HARLEY

Each family is unique when it comes to this area of their married life. Bob's and my guideline is: If the wife has a career, the money she earns should not be used on the basic support of the family. A family needs to learn to live on a budget based on the husband's income. If your wife has to work to pay the rent, buy the food, pay the utilities, your standard of living is too high and needs to be adjusted.

Why do we believe this? If the wife has to work to support the bigger home, the bigger car, the fancier vacations, she lets her husband off the hook. Then he relaxes and sets a lower standard for what he needs to do to meet the family goals and desires. It sounds unfair, but the husband needs to step up to the plate and be the main breadwinner for the family. Most often, career women want their husbands to earn enough money to allow them to feel supported and to feel that their husbands are taking care of them and their families' financial needs. Most men want to and need to provide for their families.

One of the quickest ways of earning more money each month is to spend less each month. It's a lot easier to make more money by spending less, than it is to take more advanced classes or even work overtime. If you and your wife make a "need list" and a "want list," you'll find it very helpful. The difficult part is to tell the difference between a need and a want.

Paul writes in Philippians 4:11, "Not that I speak from want, for I have learned to be content in whatever circumstances I am." That is truly one of the great secrets of life—to be content in all situations. Enjoy life at whatever stage you find yourself. If you make wise choices along life's journey, you will be blessed by the Lord. Be faithful in little things, and God will shower you with bigger things.

Investment Tips

Investing in your wife will prove to be profitable and bring lasting assets to your marriage. So...

- *treat her with respect*
- *be a good listener*
- *honor her as your wife and the mother of your children (if you have any)*
- *provide the security she needs*

Family Commitment

Most often women will have a strong desire and need to have a family. A lot of women have thought about children since they were ten years old. Taking care of a doll—changing its clothes and feeding it with a milk bottle—has prepared a woman for this role.

For men, a childhood filled with playing with Tonka trucks, digging caves, and making strange noises from their mouths hasn't prepared them for commitment to the family.

A woman's greatest desire is to have her husband come alongside her and take the leadership role in developing a strong family. As a husband, you help your wife feel loved when she sees that you too are excited about this new adventure.

A father has a very strong influence on his children—both daughters and sons. Research states over and over the effectiveness of a father's role in parenting his children. In the Old Testament in Proverbs 22:6 we read, "Train up a child in the way he should go, even when he is old he will not depart from it."

When a father is committed to this task, the wife rejoices and falls deeper in love. One exciting trend that I see in young couples is how involved the fathers are in parenting. Husbands may take a longer time in becoming committed, but once they do, they seem more involved with their children than in my generation. Much of the credit goes to having more free time in our society. In my day Dad had to work longer hours, had less time to be involved with the children, and often left raising the children to Mom, who was at home.

The old adage that families who pray together stay together is still true, but I would also add that the family who plays together also stays together. It's hard work to become a healthy, functioning family.

Men, women want to know that you are on the same team. It's easy to sit back and let your wife do all the work, but she feels really loved when she knows that you too are committed to this thing called family.

Secrets to Romancing Your Marriage

⇒ Wink and flirt with your wife at the dinner table.

⇒ "Steal" your wife's car and have it detailed for her.

≫ Make your wife a queen to your children by giving her a compliment at the dinner table.

≫ Plan a meal together for the weekend and have fun preparing it.

≫ Take her on a date and see one of her favorite movies.

13

Meeting Your Husband's Needs

*Then the LORD God said, "It is not good for the man to be
alone; I will make him a helper suitable for him."*

GENESIS 2:18

B ob, would you mind helping me move this table? I'm not strong
enough!" I love to hear Emilie say that she needs me. Her need
allows me to be what God created me to be—the stronger partner,
the protector, the provider. If I'm not allowed to help my wife, one of
my purposes as a husband is taken away from me.

Many women are assertive and very competent. The wise woman
today, however, is beginning to slow down. She has realized that
enough's enough, and she is giving up her attempt to be superwoman
and/or supermom. She has realized that the elusive goal of doing
and being all things isn't worth what it's costing her to try to reach it.
Such a woman, free of society's unrealistic expectations and its call
to be independent, can say, "Honey, I need you. Would you please
help me?"

The simple, direct statement, "I need your help" reinforces your
husband's masculinity. Most husbands won't refuse a wife's straight-
forward expression of a need. Whether your request is large or small,
ask your husband for help. The way life goes, you won't have to make
up opportunities for him to help you. We all have plenty of very real
needs that can be expressed.

In her book *Being a Woman,* clinical psychologist Toni Grant offers wives this advice:

> It is important that a man feels that he fulfills a purpose in your life, that he somehow makes the woman feel better, safer, and more beautiful than she was before. He needs to know that his masculine presence makes a difference to her feminine well being; otherwise two people may have met person to person, but not man to woman.[1]

Again and again, Scripture reminds us of the importance of having someone come alongside to help when times are difficult. Reaching out helps meet our needs and also creates a special bond with the person we let come near.

I encourage you to let your husband come near, whether your need is large or small, emotional, physical, spiritual, intellectual, or material. One of his key roles is to provide for and protect his family. When you allow your husband to do this, you bring out his masculine side. You'll probably also find yourself feeling closer to him because he has just taken care of you in some way.

Knowing and Meeting Your Mate's Needs

Women and men are often unaware of what their partners need. Why are we so blind? Perhaps because some of us are looking for what we can get, rather than what we can give in our marriage. Most of us are more than willing and ready to give—but we don't know what to give or how we can best meet our mate's needs. Emilie and I are still trying to figure this one out!

In *His Needs, Her Needs,* author Willard F. Harley, Jr., lists five basic needs husbands bring to a marriage. They are:

1. Sexual fulfillment
2. Recreational companionship
3. An attractive spouse
4. Domestic support
5. Admiration[2]

A husband benefits greatly when his wife recognizes his needs and does her best to meet these five needs.

Sexual Fulfillment

In Emilie's background, sexual intimacy was synonymous with a dull, dirty duty. Her home, dominated by a violent alcoholic father, was anything but a model of romantic love, fulfilling sex, or warm intimacy between a husband and wife. According to Emilie's early view, sex was something a couple did to have children. It was not something that was pleasurable or enjoyable. When her father died, Emilie was left without a father figure for the important teenage years of her life. So she came to our marriage without a healthy understanding of the role of love, sex, and intimacy between a husband and wife. She was first attracted to me by the gentleness and warmth she had missed in her home, but she didn't have a positive model with which to develop intimacy in our relationship.

Contrary to Emilie's experience, I was brought up by very gentle, loving parents. There were always positive expressions of love around. Sex was much more to our parents than just creating children. It was a topic that was discussed with great respect. My parents were very open with their hugs, kisses, compliments, and physical "love" pinches. They started their romancing early in the day and were ready to show the world how much they loved each other.

So on the topic of love, sex, and intimacy, Emilie and I entered our marriage relationship from two opposite poles, as different as hot and cold. And yet here we are, well into our fifth decade together as husband and wife, and more in love now than when we started. I could have "rushed and crushed" Emilie with my sexuality and openness; and she could have iced our relationship from her background that lacked intimacy. But with love, trust, and patience on both our parts, our relationship has grown into the loving, intimate partnership we enjoy today.

To promote an atmosphere of love and mutual fulfillment, we need to foster romance in our marriages. Romance leads to emotional intimacy, a key contributor to sexual intimacy. Are you a romantic wife? If not, start making phone calls to say, "I love you." Leave sexy notes for him and send thoughtful cards expressing your love in tender words. Give your mate physical attention—hold hands, touch tenderly, hug and kiss often. If your mate comes from a home that was less affectionate than yours, patiently grow together as physically romantic partners by lovingly teaching each other the magic of touch. And women, it's okay for you to initiate sexual intimacy. God gave women, as well as men, the desire for sex, so it makes sense that sometimes you will want to initiate the intimacy.

> *We pray that the young men and women of today and tomorrow will grow up with the realization that sex is a beautiful flame they carry in the lantern of their bodies.*
>
> –DEMETRIUS MONOUNOS

Another key to sexual fulfillment has to do with the sexual act itself. Having achieved sexual intimacy, many Christian couples wonder what kind of sexual intimacy is appropriate for believers. Again and again Emilie and I are asked, "Is it okay for Christian couples to…?" In response, we usually refer to Hebrews 13:4, "Let marriage be held in honor among all, and let the marriage bed be undefiled" (ESV), as the guideline to determine what kind of love-making is appropriate. Emilie and I talk to each other to see if the activity in question would enrich our intimacy. If we both feel that the activity would bring us closer together, and if both of us would enjoy it, we go ahead.

Sometimes a couple puts a certain lovemaking technique on hold because one partner is uncomfortable with the idea, and that is as it should be. We must be very sensitive to our partner's desires and not pressure him or her into doing something uncomfortable. After all, our sexuality is a gift given to promote intimacy! If you aren't sure about certain practices, apply the principle of Proverbs 3:6: "In all thy ways acknowledge him, and he shall direct thy paths" (KJV). Talk to the Lord about the proposed activity. It's amazing how God will reveal the proper answer to both of you.

Husbands and wives experience sexual fulfillment when emotional intimacy has already been achieved, when we agree on appropriate activities, and—the third key—when we are students of our mates and therefore able to meet their needs.

What better way to learn what our mate needs and enjoys than to ask questions and discuss feelings, needs, and expectations? Emilie doesn't hesitate to ask me if there is anything I would like her to do for me sexually that we aren't doing or if there is anything that I don't want her to do—and I freely ask her the same questions. Such frank discussions can eliminate assumptions and pave the way for deeper intimacy and greater sexual fulfillment. When Emilie tells me where she likes to be touched and stroked, I can more completely meet her needs and enrich our lovemaking.

Let me add a few more thoughts on sexual intimacy. I encourage you and your husband to alternate the roles of giver and receiver in foreplay and intercourse. Don't get into a rut. Keep some mystery in your sex life. The sex act alone—without romantic moments, open communication, and mutual contentment in the relationship—can become shallow and lonely. Express through verbal and nonverbal communication your wants and preferences and encourage your husband to do the same. Sex in a context of openness, trust, acceptance, and love is indeed rich and fulfilling for both partners.

God's Idea of Intimacy

The Bible's teaching on marriage has helped Emilie and me learn about God's master plan for husbands and wives. One of the most important passages we have discovered is 1 Corinthians 7:1-5:

It is good for a man not to touch a woman. Nevertheless, because of sexual immorality, let each man have his own wife, and let each woman have her own husband. Let the husband render to his wife the affection due her, and likewise also the wife to her husband. The wife does not have authority over her own body, but the husband does. And likewise the husband does not have authority over his own body, but the wife does. Do not deprive one another except with consent for a time, that you may give yourselves to fasting and prayer; and come together again so that Satan does not tempt you because of your lack of self-control (NKJV).

These verses provide four solid guidelines for couples who desire love and intimacy in their relationship.

First, be faithful to one person. Sexual immorality was rampant in the city of Corinth, the home of the church to which Paul is writing here—and our society is, sadly, quite similar to that ancient world. Christian men and women today live in a world that accepts extramarital affairs and divorce. Places of employment and the local gym are often scenes of temptation. God's Word, however, clearly commands us to be faithful to our spouse (Exodus 20:14; Matthew 5:27-32; 19:18).

Second, be available to each other. A husband is to give of himself to fulfill his wife's needs, and a wife is to give of herself to fulfill her husband's needs. We are to freely ask for and give affection to one another. Don't be afraid to tell your mate that you are in the mood for love. Always be ready to respond when your partner is in the mood. If you are too tired to enjoy each other and meet each other's needs, you may need to eliminate other commitments and activities to be the kind of spouse God calls you to be.

Third, submit to each other. Closely related to being available to our partners is being willing to submit to their sexual desires and needs. Wives, if your mate wants to make love, you should not withhold yourself from him, but submit to his desires. Be open about your own desires and your energy level so you can arrive at a mutually satisfying plan for the evening. Be aware that your willingness to meet your partner's sexual needs and desires—besides being an act of obedience to Scripture—may very well prevent him from falling into sin with someone who seems more ready to meet his needs than you are. And husbands, the same is true for you. If your wife is expressing a desire for more affection, make sure that you are taking the time to show her that she's loved.

Finally, keep on meeting your spouse's sexual needs. Paul notes that the only exception to this guideline is taking time for prayer and fasting. Other than those specified times, a husband and wife should be available to each other and always seek to meet the other's needs.

The Bible offers rich insight into the marriage relationship. Consider, for instance, that the New Testament writers liken Jesus' relationship to the church to the relationship between a

> *Marriage is a sacred vow or commitment that you both made before God, and it is a very serious matter to break that vow. God gave marriage to us for our happiness, and I believe with His help you can discover what it means to build your lives together on Christ's foundation.*
>
> —BILLY GRAHAM

husband and wife (see Ephesians 5:25). I encourage you to spend some time studying what God's Word teaches about your marriage. Knowing and following the Creator's master plan will enrich your marriage—sexually and otherwise.

Intimate Tips for Women

When Emilie talks to women about how to build intimacy in their marriages, she often directs them to the teachings of 1 Peter 3:1-6. Whether or not your husband is a believer, Emilie says, he will respond favorably if you follow these scriptural guidelines:

- Be submissive in love to your husband. Don't resist him or rebel against him. Encourage him to be the leader in the family.
- Demonstrate your Christian faith through your lifestyle. Don't preach.
- Be loyal to your husband in every way.
- Take care to remain attractive on the outside.
- Develop a quiet and gentle spirit that is inwardly attractive.
- Develop a feminine and serene style to your life.

I would add that a woman should never criticize or attack her husband. A man's outward display of strength—however irritating that display may be—is often a cover-up for feelings of insecurity. When a woman attacks her man's ego, she certainly doesn't foster the intimacy she desires in the relationship. Instead, her husband may become withdrawn and noncommunicative, angry, and resentful. He won't respond to his critical wife with sensitivity, understanding, and compassion, and he may find himself unable to perform sexually. Also he may easily be tempted by another woman who understands his needs and will build him up rather than tear him down. So instead of attacking your husband, respect him and encourage him. Your husband needs to know that he is important to you and your children. When he knows you believe in him and support him, he will be much more open and ready to be intimate with you.

Is Intimacy Possible?

Are you wondering whether real intimacy is even possible in your marriage? I assure you that it is. Genuine intimacy comes when both you and your husband are willing to submit yourselves to each other out of reverence for Christ (see Ephesians 5:21). Such mutual submission has protected Emilie and me from Satan who would have based his attacks on a prideful unwillingness to bend, accommodate, and submit to one another.

Know too that intimacy doesn't just happen. It takes persistent prayer and discipline to apply God's principles that encourage intimacy to your marriage. Again, I challenge you to study God's Word, on your own and with your spouse, to learn what He says about love, sex, and intimacy.

I also challenge you to look at yourself as honestly as you can. What qualities would make you a better wife? Where is God calling you to welcome His transforming Spirit into your heart? Ask God to help you see where you can become more the wife He wants you to be. Then prayerfully set some goals for yourself and pursue them doggedly.

Finally, continue to love the Lord with all your heart. By actively loving God and walking closely with Him, you plug yourself into His infinite and divine love, which will feed your love for your husband and foster intimacy in your marriage. Be a doer of the Word in your marriage. Let your obedience to God's commands to serve and to love one another bring new life and new closeness to your marriage. After all, God created sex and marriage, and He desires that you find love and intimacy in His creation.

Recreational Companionship

Think back to those early courting days. Do you have memories of tennis, golf, hiking, camping, and sporting events? Now that you have been married a few years and have a child or two, have you stopped doing those things? Or maybe your husband still enjoys those activities, but you are happier reading books, listening to good music, watching a good romance movie on television, or spending an evening at the theater. Or maybe you're the athlete and your husband prefers more sedentary activities. Do you remember how you and your husband used to love doing everything together? Is that still true? Or are you wondering what went wrong along the way?

Think about those couples you know who seem to have a strong marriage. They almost certainly exhibit an ability to enjoy each other's interests. And that doesn't mean that she plays tennis only and always with him or that he won't go out on the golf course without her. It means that spouses are interested and supportive of each other's recreation.

Our son, Brad, for instance, married a woman who likes to run, swim, bicycle, and exercise just as he does. She participates in many of his recreational activities. In our case, however, Emilie is not very athletic, but she does encourage and support my interest in sports. Likewise, I spend time with her doing what she enjoys—going out to dinner to celebrate a special occasion, attending the theater, or reading a book together. Emilie and I work together to give each other the freedom to enjoy our personal interests *and* to enjoy what the other person likes. Such compromise and sharing of our time keeps us growing together, something that separate vacations and long-term or frequent solo outings would not allow. In fact, such separateness can be very dangerous to a marriage relationship.

Although the media shows the boys out fishing, drinking beer, and saying, "It doesn't get better than this!" we men do want our wives to share fun and recreational activities with us. Certainly some men's activities may be riskier, sweatier, and dirtier than some women enjoy, and some women's activities may be too quiet or passive for some men. Emilie's choice of a movie, for instance, reflects her preference for softness, romance, and tenderness. I don't receive the same response to an invitation to an action movie that I do when I ask her to see a romance! Again, compromise is called for, as is balance, and recreational compromises might include lunch or dinner out, a picnic, a walk, shopping, and attending various cultural events.

At times, however, men need to be with men and women need to be with women. After all, we have different needs and we have different things to give to one another. I'm sure you know the satisfaction of "girl talk." No matter how good a listener your husband is, there is something qualitatively different about sharing the latest event with a special friend. She gives you something that your husband can't give and meets a need that your husband can't meet. Likewise, some of my male friends give me things that Emilie can't and, in doing so, meet some of my needs that Emilie can't meet (through no fault of her own). It's a fact of life that our mate is not going to meet all our needs. That's why same-sex friendships are so important to a healthy marriage.

Again, let me emphasize that balance is important. The time we spend with our spouse needs to take priority over the time we spend with our friends. Willard Harley says, "When you do things separately, you have a tendency to grow apart, each experiencing your most enjoyable moments of fun and relaxation without the other. Couples with separate recreational interests miss a golden opportunity. They often spend their most enjoyable moments in the company of someone else. It stands to reason that the person with whom you share the most enjoyable moments will give you the greatest dividends."[3]

What do these words say to you? Do they help you answer the question raised earlier: "What went wrong along the way?" Maybe as you and your husband have made choices about how to use your time, you've dropped some activities that you could be sharing. Wouldn't it be more beneficial to your marriage to find some recreational activities you can share?

An Attractive Spouse

Men value sexual fulfillment, recreational companionship, and an attractive spouse. And what is attractive? The Bible offers this answer: "Don't be concerned about the outward beauty that depends on jewelry, or beautiful clothes, or hair arrangement. Be beautiful inside, in your hearts, with the lasting charm of a gentle and quiet spirit that is so precious to God. That kind of deep beauty was seen in the saintly women of old, who trusted God and fitted in with their husband's plans" (1 Peter 3:3-5 TLB).

Scripture calls women to be godly and to develop an inward beauty, but wise women also work to make themselves pleasing to their husband's eye—and that's right on target. Now, as a woman, you might not feel that the externals are very important, but doesn't looking nice make you feel better about yourself? Furthermore, externals are important because men are sexually aroused by visual stimulation. When Emilie looks good, I look at her often and I like what I see. When men aren't proud of what they see in their wives, they become more vulnerable to having an affair. A pleasing appearance will invite your husband to touch and hold you—and no one else. Besides, your husband wants to be proud that you're by his side whether at home or in public. Every married woman needs to ask herself, "Am I looking my best when I am with my husband? Is he proud of my personal appearance?" If you feel you could make yourself more appealing and attractive, know that the resources available are many, ranging from self-help books, friends who will give suggestions, color and wardrobe seminars, and department store consultants who will assist you in developing a new you.

Domestic Support

Why is an organized, smoothly functioning home important to a man? One reason is that we need a place to unwind after a day at work. We can feel drained after solving the problems, dealing with the challenges, and feeling the stresses of the day. We need to have a moment of quiet after work. When I arrived home, I used to always say to Emilie, "You think I'm home, but I just sent my body ahead of me!" In reality I wouldn't be home for another 30 minutes. During that half hour, I regrouped. I didn't handle any emergencies or deal with any bad news. I'd often get a cold drink, sit in my favorite chair, and even take a brief nap. That time allowed me to change gears. After 30 minutes, I was truly home and able to function as a member of the family. I appreciated Emilie giving me this time to adjust, and she was able to do so because the home was functioning smoothly.

But what can be done when both spouses work outside the home? In that situation the couple needs to come up with a division of labor so that both the wife and the husband have their needs met. This division of labor often happens rather easily when a couple is first married. Then there is a lot of give-and-take because the husband is accustomed to taking care of himself in some fashion, and he usually continues along fine until the children arrive. At that point he may worry about not having enough money, take on another job, and begin to resent helping out at home. Tired from a full day, irritated by freeway traffic, and frustrated with his unappreciative boss, he comes home stressed out. If the wife also works out of the home, she has identical stresses and pressures. Such a situation can take a serious toll on a marriage relationship. But you already know that. You want answers!

A solution may come when a couple looks closely at how they are currently using their time and energy around the house. This exercise is easier when the household responsibilities are divided into four categories:[4]

1. *Income-generating activities.* Work that earns money for family living expenses falls into this category.

2. *Childcare.* All tasks dealing with feeding, dressing, supervising, and caring for your children.

3. *Household responsibilities.* Includes cooking, cleaning, washing, ironing, shopping, and organizing the home.

4. *Repair and maintenance of the home, automobile, and mechanical possessions.* Includes mowing the lawn, painting the house, repairing the car, and fixing broken toys.

Sit down with pencil and paper and list what the husband does and what the wife does. It could be surprising to discover that one of the marriage partners is doing a lot more than the other. With so many wives working out of the home, maybe she needs some help in certain areas. You might agree that the husband and children could help. You might even decide to hire someone to come to the house and help out.

One husband announced to his wife that on Mondays he was going to be responsible for the evening meal. He may make it, buy it, take the family out, or set up a picnic. He was going to relieve his wife for at least one night of dinner preparation. His wife was very excited that her husband sensed that she needed some relief in this area.

> *Most of those who aren't at home, longing to get away, are away, longing to get home.*

Couples face very real challenges when it comes to managing a home and raising a family when both husband and wife work outside the home. In fact many women are deciding to stop working outside the home to become full-time homemakers and mothers. They are realizing that's the only way they can have the kind of home—and children!—they want. And being at home allows that home to be the castle a man wants and a haven of quietness, tranquility, love, and acceptance that every family member needs.

Admiration

People have very fragile identifies. Men, especially, will go to great lengths to protect their identities as men. They must come to deeply trust a person before they will share who they really are. These facts make a man a sponge for his wife's admiration.

In all of the healthy marriages I have ever seen, the wife sincerely admires her husband—and she doesn't keep it a secret from him or anyone else! Acceptance. Adoration. Approval. Appreciation. Admiration. When we husbands receive these things from our wives, we can be confident leaders in the home, capable providers, and the men of God He calls us to be.

Your husband truly needs your admiration and approval, and the Scriptures call you to give that to him: "If you love someone...you will always believe in him, always expect the best of him" (1 Corinthians 13:7 TLB). Wives, you need to be a cheerleader for your husband. You need to yell, scream, jump, and clap for the home team. When was the last time you cheered for your husband?

It's important that you let your husband know beyond a shadow of a doubt that he is your superman, hero, and knight in shining armor.

You can do this with a phone call or personal note that says, "You are special to me! I love you and I believe in you." Make a love basket for him or plan a surprise weekend for just the two of you. These acts of love release your husband to become all God wants him to be. And this kind of admiration encourages, energizes, and motivates your husband. It also helps him stand strong against the pressures and criticisms that may come from work.

We have all heard that behind every great man is a great woman. A loving, admiring, and godly woman will indeed cause a man to gain greater stature than he would on his own. A wife's encouragement can make her husband a better man.

Admire your husband! Support him in his work and his play! Encourage him in his Christian walk! Shower him with acceptance, adoration, appreciation, and admiration! Your man wants you, his wife, to be his most enthusiastic fan. He becomes stronger and more confident from your support and encouragement.

Our Husband's Needs

Meeting your man's needs is easier when you clearly understand what they are. He needs sexual fulfillment, recreational companionship, an attractive spouse, domestic support, and your admiration. Meet these and you'll strengthen your husband *and* your marriage. And I can almost guarantee that you'll find your husband more interested in meeting your needs and being more effective in doing so. When a man is treated like a king, he in return will begin to treat you as his queen. The world says that you are to receive first, then you give; the Christian is to give first, then receive. Do the opposite of what the world says, and you will be astounded at what begins to happen. Be willing to take the risk.

Secrets to Romancing Your Marriage

⇒ Ask your husband if he has three or four specific needs that you can work toward satisfying.

⇒ Spend some time discussing each point so you understand exactly what he is saying. List these ideas in your journal. You might even want to recite them back to him to make sure you've written them down correctly.

⇒ Rank these needs by priority.

⇒ On the next day, write down in your journal specifically what you can do to fulfill his suggestions.

⇒ Pray over this "action" list, and ask God to direct your path.

⇒ Begin to implement your ideas. Remember, they don't all have to be done at once. You can spread them out over two or three months.

14

Four Marriage Health Builders

And now these three remain: faith, hope and
love. But the greatest of these is love.

1 CORINTHIANS 13:13 NIV

We all enter marriage with some idea of what a marriage is meant to be, usually based on what we observed from our own parents, church, friends, and the prevailing culture in which we are raised. But far too seldom do we take our pattern for marriage from God—the very One who designed marriage and family life in the beginning. In the Bible God offers some very basic principles for both husbands and wives. If you finish reading this book, you will be exposed to many of God's principles on this holy union—marriage between a man and a woman. Scripture does not give any other arrangements than for a man and woman to be married.

This lovely lady was called Eve, and she was formed out of one of Adam's ribs. She was designed to be Adam's helpmate. Our present day women have lost hold of this role. The politically correct crowd has attempted to tell women that they need not adhere to this principle of God's. Women are told to be assertive and combative, to be their own person and get out from under the bondage of their husbands.

What happens when this principle is violated? It becomes a battle to see which marriage partner has control of the family. It becomes a power struggle. When this happens the marriage will end in disaster. It will fall apart. The virtues of 1 Corinthians 13:13 are necessary to heal, to uplift, and to sustain a relationship. David Augsburger, in his book *Sustaining Love,* expands on these three virtues and adds a fourth—justice.

Faith is the commitment to creative fidelity; it is faithfulness to each other before God. Faith is both a way of perceiving and of acting; it is believing and doing.

Hope is the call of creative trust; it is hopelessness with each other before God. Hope is both a push from within the "hopeful" hoper and the pull from the possibilities of the future.

Love is the choice to see the other partner as equally precious; it is lovingkindness that acts in equal regard. Love is a way of seeing, feeling, thinking, and acting toward another.

Justice is the commitment to work out mutually satisfactory and visibly equitable sharing of opportunities, resources, and responsibilities in living with others; it is a creative drive for fairness in all covenantal relationships. Justice goes beyond retribution for injuries, and redistribution of resources to a redemptive and releasing discovery of what is truly right, good, and beautiful.[1]

The four marriage builders are such a valuable brick in building a solid foundation in designing a home that will endure the storms of life. Your cornerstone for your marriage will be the same as it is for the church—Jesus Christ. Remember, marriage is so important because it is built on the same principles as the church.

Secrets to Romancing Your Marriage

≫ Mend a quarrel.

≫ Search out a forgotten friend.

≫ Dismiss a suspicion and replace it with trust.

≫ Write a letter to someone you miss.

≫ Encourage a person who has lost their faith.

- ≋ Keep a promise—do what you say you are going to do.
- ≋ Forget an old grudge.
- ≋ Examine your demands on others and vow to reduce them.
- ≋ Express your gratitude.
- ≋ Overcome an old fear.
- ≋ Take a moment and appreciate the beauty of nature.
- ≋ Tell others you love them and tell them again, again, and again.

15

Keep Listening and Talking

Dear brothers, don't ever forget that it is best to
listen much, speak little, and not become angry.

JAMES 1:19 TLB

Marriage experts tell us that one of the number one causes for divorce in America today is a lack of communication. Everyone was born with one mouth and two ears—the basic tools for communication. But evidently possessing the physical tools for communication is not enough. Couples must learn how to use their mouths and ears properly for true communication to take place. Because God created marriage for companionship, completeness, and communication, we can be sure that He will also provide us with the resources for fulfilling His design.

There are three partners in a Christian marriage—husband, wife, and Jesus Christ. For healthy communication to exist between husband and wife, there must be proper communication between all three partners. If there is a breakdown in dialog between any two members, the breakdown will automatically affect the third member of the partnership. Dwight Small says, "Lines open to God invariably open to one another, for a person cannot be genuinely open to God and closed to his mate... God fulfills His design for Christian marriage when lines of communication are first opened to Him."[1] If you and your mate are having difficulty communicating, the first area to check is your individual devotional life with God.

Whenever Emilie and I suffer a breakdown in relating to one another, it is usually because one of us is not talking with God on a regular basis. When both of us are communicating with God regularly through prayer and the study of His Word, we enjoy excellent communication with each other. As the following diagram suggests, the closer Emilie and I get to God, the closer we grow together as a couple. The inverse principle is also true: The farther we move away from God by not communicating with Him, the farther apart we will be from our mates.

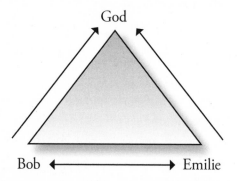

The next diagram illustrates a similar principle by using a cross. The vertical line represents our relationship to God and the horizontal line represents our relationship to others, including our mates. If the horizontal relationships are shaky and about to collapse, it is usually because our vertical relationship to God is weak.

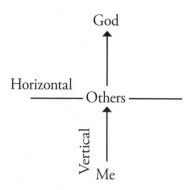

What Is Communication?

In his book *Communication: Key to Your Marriage,* Norm Wright gives an excellent definition of communication: "Communication is a process (either verbal or nonverbal) of sharing information with another person in such a way that he understands what you are saying. *Talking* and *listening* and *understanding* are all involved in the process of communication."[2]

1. *Have you already stopped listening?* With some couples, one or both partners have already stopped listening to the other. They block out everything their mates say by hiding behind a newspaper or working long and late. If you find yourself shouting at your mate to be heard, you are probably married to someone who has stopped listening.

When your mate stops listening to you, you will probably react by either withdrawing and talking less or overcompensating and talking louder and longer. Neither reaction is productive in the long run. If your mate is not listening to you, it may be because you are not communicating at a level that invites your mate's participation. In his book *Why Am I Afraid to Tell You Who I Am?* John Powell lists five levels of communication, each one deeper and more meaningful than the last. Try to identify the level you and your mate most commonly employ, then seek to improve your communication by moving to deeper levels.

Level five is *cliché conversation,* which includes everyday, casual conversation based on safe, surface statements like "How are you?"

> *Don't speak evil against each other, dear brothers and sisters. If you criticize and judge each other, then you are criticizing and judging God's law.*
>
> JAMES 4:11 NLT

"How's your family?" "Where have you been?" "I like your suit." Lacking depth, cliché conversation barely acknowledges that the other person is alive.

Level four is *reporting the facts about others.* At this level you are quoting others instead of giving personal commentary: "It will be a sunny day"; "The Orioles lost their twentieth straight game"; "The score of the football game was 17-6." There is little or no emotion or commitment at this level.

Level three, *my ideas and judgments,* is where real communication begins. Here you are willing to step out and risk expressing a personal opinion in order to be part of the decision-making process. You may feel insecure at this level, but at least you are willing to take a chance. Persons who are threatened at this level often retreat to the higher levels of communication.

Level two is *my feelings, my emotions.* At this level we express how we feel about the facts, ideas, and judgments expressed at higher levels. We may say, "I feel so much better when the sun is shining." Information is not enough at this level. Feelings must be shared in order to communicate.

Level one encompasses *complete emotional and personal truthful communication.* This level of communication requires complete openness and honesty, and involves great risk. All deep and enriching relationships operate at this level. It takes a great deal of trust, love, and understanding to communicate truthfully. This level is not a dumping ground, but a place where each partner treats the other with love and concern.[3]

Use the following questions to help you evaluate the present communication level in your marriage:

* What level of communication is most common to you and your partner?
* What are the indicators of your communication level?
* What actions can you take to move your communication to a deeper level?

If you as a couple have stopped listening to each other, here are some helpful tips we have learned about listening, which you should take to heart:

- Realize that everyone has a basic need to be listened to and heard.

- Listen intently when your partner is talking to you. Don't just think about your answers. Listening is more than politely waiting your turn to speak.

- Listen objectively. Put down the newspaper, turn off the television, look your partner in the eye, and pay attention.

- Reach out and care about what's being said. Listening is active participation, not passive observance.

- Move past the surface message and get to the heart of what is being said. Listening is more than hearing words.

- Discipline yourself to listen. Listening doesn't come naturally or easily to any of us. Most of us are more comfortable when we are in control and speaking.

- Receive and process the message sent. Try to understand what is being said. At times the message may be painful, but you will be stretched if you continue to listen.

Timing is an important element in the success of communication. Honor your mate by selecting the best times to talk, listen, and understand. Emilie always allowed me the first 15 to 30 minutes after I arrived home from work to unwind. We didn't bring up difficult topics at that time unless there was an emergency. We reserved mealtimes for pleasant, edifying, and uplifting conversation. Serious topics were saved until after the pangs of hunger had been satisfied. Then, between dinner and bedtime, we covered more serious issues.

If you have a very serious topic to address, you might want to secure a babysitter and invite your mate out to dinner, so you can talk away from the distractions at home.

2. *Do you presume or judge as you listen?* As a father, I can recall many times when our children would come to me asking permission to do something or to go somewhere. Often I would start shaking my head no before they would finish asking their questions. This was a great disservice to them because I was telling them their opinions and requests were unimportant before they had time to fully express them. The answer may still have been no, but they would have accepted and understood better if I had listened to their requests, discussed them, and then given my answer.

Proverbs 18:13 says, "What a shame—yes, how stupid!—to decide before knowing the facts!" (TLB). For our mates and children to realize that we value their input, we must thoroughly hear them out before giving a response or pronouncing a judgment. This is especially important when the subject under discussion is of little interest to you. As a husband you must welcome the news of your wife's day, especially when the children are young. Words like diapers, doctors, shots, crawling, mess, and nerves all have meaning to your wife. If they are important to her, then they must become important to you, even if they have little meaning to you.

We made it a habit to take our children with us when we looked for a new home, new car, sporting equipment, stereo, and other items of family interest. We wanted them to give us input on these purchases, and we disciplined ourselves to listen to their comments acceptingly. Many times their suggestions proved to be very helpful in our final selections. But they never would have given them if we hadn't carefully listened to them.

3. *Do you touch when you listen?* Touching is probably the best way to tell your mate that you are listening to him or her. The amount of encouragement and affirmation that can be communicated through touch is astounding. Often no words are needed when there is a hug, a hand clasp, an arm around the shoulder, or even a playful pinch. Sometimes your mate just wants to be held or caressed reassuringly. They are crying out, "Are you listening? Do you care?" Your touch assures them that you are in tune with what they are saying.

4. *Are you a gut-level listener?* Gut-level listeners are intense listeners. They focus beyond what their mates *say* to hear what their mates *mean.* They are open and compassionate, asking in-depth questions and ready to communicate at level one on Powell's list. Without gut-level listening, we often miss the real meaning of the words being spoken. We must learn to listen more with our heart and soul than with our ears.

> *A fool thinks he needs no advice, but a wise man listens to others.*
>
> PROVERBS 12:15 TLB

5. *Do you take time to listen?* Communication doesn't happen by itself. You must plan for it and spend both quality-time and quantity-time doing it. If you don't have time for your mate and your children, you are too busy. C.R. Lawton said, "Time is the one thing that can never be retrieved. One may lose and regain a friend; one may lose and regain money; opportunity spurned may come again; but the hours that are lost in idleness can never be brought back to be used in gainful pursuits." And time spent listening to our mates and our children is time well spent.

A long time ago we decided that our kids were more important than other activities. Now we are glad we made that commitment of time to our kids. We realize what a blessing they are.

You will either give your time now or later to your kids. If you don't take time to listen to them and care for them now, you will be forced to spend time picking up the pieces of their insecure lives later.

Understanding

While vacationing in Mexico, we went into a neighborhood restaurant for dinner. Our waiter didn't speak English very well, but he wrote our order on his pad, and then looked us in the eye and said, "*Sí.*" We were sure he understood our order because of his affirmative response. However, when he returned with our dinner—or what he thought we had ordered for dinner—we couldn't help laughing at the missed communication.

We may speak clearly and our mates may listen intently, but if they don't understand the message, we haven't communicated very well. There are two major reasons why we fail to communicate this way. First, when we speak there is often a difference between what we mean to say and what we really say. The idea may be clear in your head, but the words you choose to express the idea may be inappropriate.

Second, when we listen there is a difference between what we hear and what we think we hear. Perhaps the words you heard correctly conveyed the speaker's idea to everyone else, but you misunderstood them. And every time you respond to what you think you heard instead of what was actually said, the communication problem is further compounded.

One way to help clarify your communication is to repeat to your

Too many of us have not learned to listen.
Poor listeners range all the way from the
impatient type—"That's nothing! Wait'll you hear
what I've done!"—to the person so absorbed
in his own thoughts that he is not aware that some-
one has spoken. Learning to listen actively and
constructively is as important as learning to speak,
if communication is to be effective.

–William C. Tacey

mate what you heard, and then ask, "Is that what you said?" Whenever you stop to ask that clarifying question, you are helping to keep the channels of understanding wide open and flowing.

If Emilie is reporting an event to someone in my hearing, and she says it happened at five o'clock when I thought it happened at six o'clock, I will immediately ask, "Five o'clock or six o'clock?" When it's all said and done, does it really make a difference if all the facts are told right? Usually not! That's why "five o'clock or six o'clock" has meant so much to us. Emilie had a favorite aunt and uncle who never could agree upon each other's version of what occurred. If one said they flew, the other would disagree and say, "No, we drove." If one said they had steak, the other one would say, "No, it was barbecued chicken." When the evening was over and we were driving home in the car, we would smile and say, "Five o'clock or six o'clock, what difference does that make?"

We know couples who argue about the slightest details when relaying a story. Who cares? It doesn't make any difference in the large life picture. Major on the majors and not the minors.

How to Communicate Better

In her book *After Every Wedding Comes a Marriage,* Florence Littauer reviews what men and women are looking for in communication. Being aware of your mate's general needs in this area will help you better communicate with him or her.

According to Littauer, men want four things: 1) Sincerity—They want to know that the topic is important to you; 2) Simplicity—They want to hear the simple facts and get to the point; 3) Sensitivity—They will open up better at the right time and the right place; and 4) Stability—They want to keep their composure and not fall apart during communication.

Women have four different wants: 1) Attention—They want their mate's full attention when they speak; 2) Agreement—They want no arguments to break down the walls between them and their mates; 3) Appreciation—They want their mates to value them and their role;

and 4) Appointments—They want their mates to honor the time and place for communication.[4]

Let me share a few additional tips that Emilie and I have successfully applied to our communication as husband and wife:

- *Be willing to change.* If you have been guilty of hindering communication in your family, you are not locked into that behavior. Ask God and your family members to forgive you for your failure. Then learn from your mistakes and change your communication pattern. Tomorrow is a new day.

- *It's okay to disagree, but not to disrespect.* Always maintain respect and honor for your mate when communicating your differences. Don't belittle, slander, or attack your partner, even in a heated exchange.

- *It takes effort to communicate well.* When you decide to communicate better, be aware that your decision is only the beginning. It takes a lot of effort from both partners to grow as good communicators. Communication is a matter of will and work.

- *Don't second-guess your partner.* Sit on your hands, keep your mouth shut, and hear your partner out, even if it takes several hours for him or her to communicate.

Solving Communication Breakdown

There are many reasons for communication breakdown between partners—perhaps as many reasons as there are couples. But there seem to be several problems that afflict many couples. Maybe you will recognize some familiar communication problems in your marriage from the list of statements below:

- I am afraid you will laugh at me.
- I know my opinion doesn't matter to you.
- I am afraid of your reaction.
- I talk so much that you stop listening.
- I know you will correct me or prove me wrong.

- I get too depressed to talk sometimes.
- I get angry too easily when we talk.
- I don't like serious conversations, so I make jokes when we talk.
- I am afraid of the silence between us.
- I don't like it when you interrupt me.
- I am afraid we won't agree.
- I am afraid you will make fun of me or my ideas.
- I always feel defensive when we talk.[5]

If you and your mate want to prevent or repair a communication breakdown, you must identify the problem areas and plan a program to overcome them. In some cases the barriers to communication may be so great that you need to seek a trained Christian counselor. Until the barriers are broken down, you will never be able to respond to your mate properly.

Following the example in space number one, list some of your real or potential communication barriers below on the left. Then determine some actions you will take to prevent or repair each problem and write your ideas on the right:

Communication Problems	Actions for Improvement
1. I am afraid of your reaction.	1. Take the risk to pray about my approach. Choose the right time and share how I feel when he/she talks about a difficult situation.
2. _____	2. _____

3. _____   3. _____

_____

_____

_____

_____

4. _____   4. _____

_____

_____

_____

_____

5. _____   5. _____

_____

_____

_____

_____

Christian marriage and family counselor Norm Wright says that many of us don't communicate because we don't believe that Christ accepts us as we are. And because we don't feel accepted by Christ, we do not accept ourselves, and we cannot accept others and communicate with them. We are too busy trying to shape up for God so that He will love us and accept us.

> *Looking for the solution without listening to the problem is working in the dark.*

The good news, of course, is that God has already accepted us because of our relationship to Jesus Christ. We don't need to prove anything to Him. We simply need to accept and reflect His love by accepting ourselves and others. Acceptance opens all the doors that lead to communication.

As I mentioned at the beginning of the chapter, communication between Christian marriage partners is a spiritual exercise. The closer you each get to God, the closer you can get to each other. Perhaps you are not communicating well as a couple because you have never opened the lines of communication between yourselves and God. Each of you must initiate the conversation with God by asking Him to come into your life in the person of His Son Jesus Christ. Then seek out a church where you can grow in your relationship to Christ. As your communication with God blossoms, you will enjoy increasingly better communication with each other.

Secrets to Romancing Your Marriage

⇝ Never vacuum during the fourth quarter of the football game.

⇝ Laugh at his jokes.

⇝ Discuss your expectations as a couple.

⇝ Listen to her stories of the past.

⇝ Allow her to grieve over her losses.

⇝ Be accountable to each other.

⇝ Choose to love your spouse today.

⇝ Don't expect to understand each other completely.

16

Men Are Weird

How blessed is the man who has made the
LORD his trust, and has not turned to the proud,
nor to those who lapse into falsehood.

PSALM 40:4

As we have traveled all over America giving seminars, Bob and I often get the same question: "Why does my husband puzzle and exasperate me as a woman?" Let's face it...men are really weird in the eyes of a woman. Who but a man

- insists that he can hear you when you are talking to him, even though he's watching TV and reading the newspaper?
- dares to ask why you're always late getting ready for church, when he only has to get himself ready, but you make breakfast and get the three children ready?
- won't stop and ask for directions even when lost?
- seems to always take the longest route to run errands?
- insists on eating unhealthy food because he likes his bread, potatoes, gravy, and roast beef?
- lectures the children about using good manners but drinks his soup from the bowl?
- worries you by working too hard but relaxes when you desperately need his help around the house?

Certainly husbands can be confusing in certain areas of your married life; yet, I find them to be very kind, comforting, attentive, and willing to please their wives. One thing is clear about most husbands, they seem unable to understand their own wives' needs and won't do much about them if they do.

A humorist once told of a conversation God had with Adam, His first creation:

> God saw that Adam enjoyed the Garden of Eden and all of its beauty, but he was looking sad and knew that something was missing from his life. God approached Adam and said, "Adam, you have been so faithful here in the garden, I would like to grant you one wish." Adam excitedly knew his wish and said, "God, I would like you to build me a bridge that would stretch from Southern California to Hawaii."
>
> God pondered the wish for a moment, and then told Adam that it was impossible to build such a bridge—an engineering impossibility. However, since He was not able to grant that wish, He told Adam that he could have another wish.
>
> Without hesitation, Adam requested from God, "God, when you give me a wife, would it also be possible to give me a handbook on how to understand women?"
>
> God frowned a little bit, and then He uttered these words, "Do you want a two-lane or four-lane bridge to Hawaii?"

Stand aside while he assembles his new "toy" without suggesting that he read the instructions.

That's a funny story and we laugh, but unfortunately it is often true. We women can be hard to figure out. We are all uniquely created and very different from men. My Bob tells me when he thinks he has me figured out, I change.

At our seminars I often speak of my husband as "my Bob." I do it to honor his position as my husband and to tell other women to leave him alone because he's mine—keep your hands off. Men, even though you can be weird at times, you at least have the hope found in Scripture. You can see what God has to say about your role in marriage.

Husbands, you can be as weird as you want, if you show the maturity in your love for your Lord and your wife. A godly woman is turned on when her man loves the Lord more than he does his wife. When a husband is in love with God, he will find it easy to be in love with his wife—the two go hand in hand with each other.

I am so blessed to have my Bob in my life. In our marriage he reflects the love that he has for God. Often women will come up to me and ask if they can take him home with them. His male friends want to punch him in the nose for raising the bar so high. Is he perfect? Far from it. After 52 years of marriage, I still scratch my head at times because he is so weird. But he is a man who wants to improve

> *Husbands, love your wives, just as Christ also loved the church and gave Himself up for her.*
>
> EPHESIANS 5:25

in his role as a husband, father, and grandfather. If Scripture gives him a principle for life, he wants to incorporate it into his life. Who is the winner in all of this? Me, the children, and the grandchildren.

Susanna Wesley, the mother of the eighteen-century evangelists Charles and John Wesley, once observed, "There are two things to do about the gospel: believe it, behave it." The easier part is to believe it; the harder part is to behave it. And that may be true of your wedding vows. The easier part is to believe the promises you made; the harder part is to act on these promises. When we do act on these promises, we show the world how much we believe in the gospel and in our marriage vows.

Marriage—with its stresses, trials, and inescapable closeness to another person—is certainly a test to see how we live out the gospel.

In marriage we have every opportunity to share the fruit of the Spirit (Galatians 5:22-23) with our spouse. All that God asks us to do and to be as His husband or wife can be—and should be—lived out within the marriage relationship.

When we honor our wedding vows, marriage can indeed be a wonderful blessing.

Sometimes our weird husbands are so hardheaded that you think they come from a stone quarry. But remember all the beautiful buildings, roads, bridges, and gardens that are built with materials made out of stone. Your marriage takes a lot of effort to have it function in a wholesome and healthy fashion.

> *I like not only to be loved, but to be told that I am loved; the realm of silence is large enough beyond the grave.*
>
> —GEORGE ELIOT

I find that today's young women have too many expectations for marriage. They have seen too many movies, read too many romance books, and have talked to too many other women who have the wrong ideas about marriage. Marriage is not always having a picture-perfect day with your wonderful lover. There are hard times, in marriage and in life, when your heart won't be throbbing and your hormones won't be pumping the love juices to the brain.

However, achieving anything of worth takes plenty of perspiration and a terrific use of physical, emotional, mental, and spiritual fortitude.

What do you do if you have that husband who is not a Christian or one who is a Christian but you just don't understand him? This next verse is not popular in today's culture, but I've seen it to be true all during my Christian walk as a wife. It is found in 1 Peter 3:1-2:

You wives, be submissive to your own husbands so that even
if any of them are disobedient to the word, they may be won
without a word by the behavior of their wives, as they observe
your chaste and respectful behavior.

An unsaved husband can better be won to Christianity by seeing
it work in his wife's godly life than by always hearing about it from
her lips.

Realize that wives will not always understand their husbands—nor
will husbands be able to always understand their wives. Don't let Satan
cause you to let a wedge come between you and your husband. If God
would have wanted us to be able to understand each other, He would
have made us all alike. Because we are different, we each bring to this
wonderful thing called marriage an excitement that takes a lifetime
to figure out. Wouldn't life be boring if we were all alike? Prize your
husband's weirdness and remember that he is a child of God.

Secrets to Romancing Your Marriage

- "Grow old along with me! The best is yet to be."–Robert
  Browning
- A gift is something that you know the receiver wants.
- Let flowers, stuffed animals, greeting cards, songs, and
  minivacations speak love for you.
- Experience the afterglow of romance. Your mate appre-
  ciates you more, is nicer to you, and is more likely to
  respond in kind.
- Romance is the expression of your love for your spouse.

17

Women Are Strange

*My most brilliant achievement was my ability to be
able to persuade my wife to marry me.*

–WINSTON CHURCHILL

We've often heard this expression from men, "I can't live with her
and I can't live without her." You can't quite figure out what you
want because you can't quite figure out your wife. You want her to be
just like you and she's not. Men, we are weird, and women are strange.
They will always do the unexpected. You want to go one way, and she
wants to go another. She wants to talk for hours on the phone, and you
want to get to the question by saying, "What's up?" Five minutes on
the phone for you is long enough, but she has 25,000 words to speak
each day (with cell phones, her need has jumped to 35,000). You like
to have a few close friends, but she can accommodate many. You are
single-task oriented—she can multitask four to five things at a time.
When a man goes to the restroom while dining out, he goes alone, but
the wife announces to all the women, "Does anyone need to go to the
ladies' room?" Inevitably three or four ladies go with her.

Have you ever noticed that men tell you how much they spent for
a tool, but a woman tells you how much she saved on her purchases?
Yes, women are strange. About the time I think I have Emilie figured
out, she changes.

I know that God has made women strange for some good reason,
but I haven't been able to figure it out yet. One thing I do know is that

DON'T QUIT

When things go wrong, as they sometimes will,

When the road you're trudging seems all uphill,

When the funds are low and the debts are high,

And you want to smile but you have to sigh,

When care is pressing you down a bit,

Rest if you must, but don't you quit.

Life is strange with its twists and turns

As every one of us sometimes learns;

And many a failure turns about

When he might have won had he stuck it out.

Don't give up though the pace seems slow;

You may succeed with another blow!

Success is failure turned inside out,

The silver tint of the clouds of doubt;

And you never can tell just how close you are,

It may be near when it seems so far.

So stick to the fight when you're hardest hit;

It's when things seem worst that you mustn't quit.

—Author Unknown

their strangeness has made me become a better student of observation. I know what makes her tick and what makes her ticked. Men, this is a very important thing to learn. Your wife might say to you someday, "You need to get with the program!" and your response will be, "What program?" See, we don't know that our wives have a program, but they do. If husbands are to survive this thing called marriage, we have to realize that our wives have a program.

What might start out to be a situation that divides you because of your differences can actually become a blessing. Consider these differences to be strengths that make your weaknesses strong. Satan would love to take these misunderstandings and divide your love for each other. He loves to make little things into big issues—issues so big that they will destroy your marriage.

Building Your Mate Up

We often are tempted to throw up our hands and say, "Why do I even try to understand him/her? When I think I know what to do, they tell me I'm wrong." Don't let this get you down. Use the opportunity to grow in your understanding of patience and of your mate.

Making a positive effect on your partner is one of the exciting parts of marriage. Remember, you are the mirror that reflects how your spouse feels about

> *Good humor is a tonic for mind and body. It is the best antidote for anxiety and depression. It is a business asset. It attracts and keeps friends. It lightens human burdens. It is the direct route to serenity and contentment.*
>
> —Grenville Kleiser

himself or herself. What they see in your facial expressions and what they see in your body language have a huge impact on who they think they are. If they receive good stuff, they will think good stuff and vice versa. It's much better to live with being upbeat than being downbeat.

Don't let a weird husband or strange wife set the course for your day. God made us so different from each other. We only seem different because each of our glasses of expectation are tinted differently—his male and yours female. When Bob doesn't understand my thought process or my response to a certain situation, he will often comment, "Oh, that's just a girl thing!" What he is really telling me is that he doesn't understand, he would have responded differently, and he would have used different words, but that's okay. You are a woman, thus you can do things differently, and that's okay. Bob is really my best encourager, even if he doesn't always understand why I might do something. I am Bob's best cheerleader, even though he is weird. We are both content in who we are.

Keep a Good Sense of Humor

Laughter and kidding are great tools in defusing these differences. We have learned through the years not to take each other so seriously. A long time ago we decided to be friends and partners. We are on the same team. Laughter is a great tool to make a tense situation bearable. The inflection of your voice changes when you are able to laugh. Somehow laughter breaks through the stresses of tension. Be cool at all times, count to ten, take ten deep breaths. Do whatever you need to express to the other person that they are acceptable.

Me and Her
She is compulsive,
I am impulsive,
She likes it hot,
I like it cold.

She is neat,
I'm a slob.
Andy Rooney says, "A's marry Z's,"
But we are in different alphabets.
I push,
She pulls.
She says, "Down."
I say, "Up."
She is night,
I am day.
Living together is hard.
Living without her would be impossible.

–AUTHOR UNKNOWN

Secrets to Romancing Your Marriage

- Do a Saturday chore together.
- When you are angry with him or her, talk it out—don't give the silent treatment.
- Wear a piece of jewelry he bought for you that you haven't worn for a while.
- Cut some flowers for the home.
- Light a few candles and place them on the dinner table. Remember to dim the lights.
- Do what you say you are going to do.
- Repeat back to your mate what he or she said, making sure you understood what was said.

18

Making Your Wife Your Best Friend

*The LORD God said, "It is not good for the man to be
alone. I will make a helper suitable for him."*

GENESIS 2:18 NIV

O ne of the true strengths of a man is when he selects a lady to
be his wife and then lives up to his wedding vows that he will
love her until death. Paul, in Ephesians 5:25, writes, "Husbands, love
your wives, just as Christ also loved the church and gave himself up
for her" (NIV). All that most women want is to know their husbands
love them.

When God created the first woman and wife, He also created
Adam's first friend. A wife is to be her husband's friend. Emilie has
certainly been mine. What does God intend for a married couple?
Let's look closely at Scripture.

- God gives the woman to the man to be "a helper suitable for
  him" (Genesis 2:18 NIV). How is your wife your helper? How
  does she help you at work? At home? Does she seem to often
  know what you need or want before you ask? How often do
  you let her know that you appreciate her helpfulness?

- God creates woman from man's rib (Genesis 2:21-22). In Genesis 1:27, we learn that God created human beings in His image.
  The fact that each of us is created in God's image calls us to
  honor and respect one another. What do you do to show your

wife that you honor and respect her? How do you show and tell your wife that you love her?

- Adam perceived Eve as part of his own bone and own flesh (Genesis 2:23). If I recognize that Emilie is actually part of me, I will want to treat her as well as I treat myself. I will want to take good care of her and provide for her every need. What selfish behavior do you need to apologize for and change? What could you do to take better care of your wife?

In close friendship nothing is hidden. Such friendship is built on trust. This friendship takes time to grow and develop. What better context for this kind of friendship to grow than in your marriage? How does your marriage measure up?

I have found that wives will feel loved when they experience these four A's:

> *I've had the boyhood thing of being Elvis. Now I want to be with my best friend, and my best friend's my wife. Who could ask for anything more?*
>
> —John Lennon

- Adoration
- Appreciation
- Acceptance
- Affection

Your love grade will grow tremendously when your wife knows and experiences these four qualities of love.

Adoration

Webster's college dictionary defines this word as "a worshiping or paying homage as to a divinity; great love, devotion and respect." A husband can show this kind of favor to his wife by letting her know that she is loved for who she is in God's eyes. You have a love for her as your wife. You proudly introduce her to your friends as your wife. You respect her so much that you encourage her to be all that God wants her to be. Your relationship to her is not one of competition but one of completion. Your strengths strengthen her weaknesses; in turn her strengths strengthen your weaknesses. Together you make a great team.

Appreciation

A woman always loves to hear the words "I love you," but she also loves to hear that you appreciate all that she does for you and the family. She can't hear the following comments often enough:

- That was a great dinner.
- Thanks for washing and ironing my shirts. They always look so neat and clean.
- I appreciate how good of a steward you are with our finances.
- I love your new hairstyle.
- That blue dress brings out the color of your eyes.

Whether she is a stay-at-home mom or a wife who works out of the home, women love to hear you say "I appreciate all you do."

Acceptance

So often adults want to change people. "If they would only be like me, they would be okay," we say. Do this, do that. Change, change, change. The "natural man" wants to change those around us. A great way to find favor is to love someone just the way he or she is. Don't go into a relationship thinking that you will change your mate when you get married. You married her the way she is so be satisfied if she stays that way.

A woman feels very secure when she knows in her heart that you accept her. Any changes are going to come through the leading and conviction of the Holy Spirit. Say over and over again, "I love you just the way you are."

Affection

Giving affection is a signal that you adore, you appreciate, and you accept your wife. A woman often doesn't have to have the whole love scene to feel affection between her and her husband. As men we think once we start showing affection it must climax to the end. Women, on the other hand, appreciate a sweet word, a small gift, a squeeze on the shoulder, putting your arm around her on the couch, rubbing her feet with a fragrant body lotion, holding hands as you walk in the park.

> *You might be the head of the family, but your wife is the neck that turns the head.*

Men, if you start doing these little forms of affection, I will guarantee you that your romance thermometer will explode. Try it and you'll see what happens.[1]

Secrets to Romancing Your Marriage

- ⇒ Give your wife a gift certificate for a one-hour facial or massage (or both).
- ⇒ Tell your wife that you will take her and the family out for dinner tomorrow night.
- ⇒ Invite your wife to the movies—and see one of the movies she's been talking about.
- ⇒ Give your wife a foot massage with some good spa oil or body cream.

≫ Help your wife clean up the kitchen after dinner.

≫ Ask your wife to make up a "honey do" list for you. Specify no more than five items though.

≫ Take your wife to her favorite restaurant (no children this time).

≫ Give your wife a coupon that's good for ten hours of free time while you watch the kids.

19

Money Matters in a Great Marriage

*You must never think that you have made
yourselves wealthy by your own power and strength.
Remember that it is the LORD your God who
gives you the power to become rich.*

DEUTERONOMY 8:17-18 TEV

Emilie and I began married life with $500 in the bank and an annual teacher's salary of $3,600—take-home pay was $247 per month. We sat down at the dining room table on the first of each month and paid the bills. Sometimes there was too much month left at the end of our money. But neither of us came from wealthy families, so we were content to begin at this level. Any money we had received while growing up was earned by hard work—Emilie worked in her mother's dress shop and I worked paper routes and odd jobs around the neighborhood. We each brought to our marriage a solid work ethic and a responsible approach to saving and spending money.

Emilie and I have successfully continued our disciplines for handling money for more than 52 years. We have always agreed on our budgets and purchases. We have regularly given back to the Lord what He has so abundantly given us. We have maintained a disciplined savings habit. We have never lost control of our credit. And we have established an investment program which includes life insurance, stocks, bonds, and real estate. In this chapter we want to share with you some fundamentals for money management we have learned and practiced.

Good Money Management Is Imperative

For the Christian family, good money management is imperative for at least three reasons. First, God associates our ability to handle spiritual matters with our ability to handle money. In Luke 16:11, Jesus stated, "If you have not been trustworthy in handling worldly wealth, who will trust you with true riches?" (NIV). If we want to grow in spiritual responsibility and blessing, we must prove our faithfulness in the area of financial responsibility. God is not going to trust us spiritually if we have been irresponsible with our money.

Second, financial responsibility is important because we are only caretakers of what really belongs to God. Psalm 24:1 declares, "The earth is the LORD's, and all it contains." You may *possess* many things—home, car, furniture, boat, money—but you don't *own* anything. Even your ability to earn money comes from God (see Deuteronomy 8:17-18). Everything belongs to Him. You are merely a steward of His property. God holds you personally responsible to faithfully manage for Him whatever money or possessions He allows you to have.

Often we are tempted to grasp our possessions selfishly as if they belonged to us and not to God. I'll never forget the beautiful blue 1972 Mercedes Benz I cherished for about ten years. I waxed it often to keep it shining brightly, kept it in the garage when I wasn't driving it, and dusted it every day.

Once when Emilie and I were away for a few days, our son, Brad, and a few buddies came home from college to go skiing. Brad saw my Mercedes in the garage and decided to take it to the mountains to impress his friends and any young ladies they might meet. He strapped the ski rack to the roof, loaded the skis and poles onto the rack, and headed for the slopes.

All went well until they started home. The ski rack vibrated loose and slid off, leaving a dent and a large scratch on the roof of my Mercedes. When I returned home, Brad broke the news. When I saw my damaged car, I was mad at Brad for taking my car without asking and devastated that he had allowed my prized car to be damaged. But it took me only a moment to regain my composure. God was using the incident to test my perspective on my car. "Gee, God, Your car has a scratch and a dent," I said. I drove God's Mercedes for another year and a half with the scratched and dented roof. Each time I looked at the damage, it reminded me who really owned the car.

As caretakers of God's money and property, we must obediently grow and nurture the spiritual fruit of self-control (see Galatians 5:22-23). Every couple we have counseled over the years regarding money problems had at least one member who lacked self-control. Money problems were just one of many undisciplined areas in their lives, including maintenance of the home, yard, and automobile, spiritual life, personal hygiene, children, and on and on. These couples exemplify the "easy come, easy go" generation. They are irresponsible with their money and possessions and, consequently, always have problems in these areas. God wants to give to us abundantly, but He also wants us to exercise self-control over the management of what He gives.

> *A faithful man will abound with blessings.*
>
> PROVERBS 28:20 NIV

Third, financial responsibility is necessary to help us avoid a number of major money mistakes. Most couples fall into one or more of the following traps because they have not appropriated biblically based principles for the use of their money and possessions:

1. *Getting into debt beyond your means to repay.* We live in the now generation, and we don't like to save for something when we can buy it now on credit. But easily available credit can become a problem when we have no predetermined limits and guidelines for spending. I am not saying that you shouldn't go into debt. But undisciplined credit spending is a big mistake (see Romans 13:8).

2. *Living a money-centered life.* It is easy in our culture to

get caught up in the pursuit of wealth and material possessions. But Scriptures such as Matthew 6:19-24 and 1 Timothy 6:6-10 warn us that God is to be our focus, not money. Without careful, prayerful money management, we can be overly influenced by our money-centered society.

3. *Trying to get rich quick.* Once a reputable Christian man in our church urged me to buy some stock at $26 per share, promising me it could be sold at $40 per share within a month. I eagerly invested a large sum of money, only to lose it all when the "sure-fire" company went bankrupt. My overeagerness to make a financial killing cost us dearly. Proper money management will help you keep tantalizing schemes like these in perspective (see Proverbs 28:22).

4. *Withholding benevolence.* According to Proverbs 11:24-25, if we give generously to God and others, we will receive everything we need. But we often turn that principle around by grabbing and holding onto everything we need and want, and giving only from the leftovers—if there are any. For the Christian, being a grabber instead of a giver is not only unscriptural, it is financially unprofitable.

5. *Using people.* When money becomes a priority in our lives, our relationships often suffer. We use people as stepping-stones to promotions or personal gain, or we see people as our customers instead of those we are to love, honor, and care for. We are in trouble when we scramble the saying "Love people and use things" to read "Use people and love things."

6. *Misplacing priorities.* When we overemphasize money in our lives, we try to beat God's system and do things our

way. The order of the big three priorities in life—God, family, and work—often gets wrongly aligned to read:

Work, family, God
or work, God, family
or family, work, God
or family, God, work
or God, work, family
until we finally get it right:
God, family, work.

At one point in my working experience, I had to ask myself this very basic question: How much of my soul am I going to sell to my boss? Until I answered, "No more," I was never satisfied because I was letting other people establish my priorities. When I took control of my life, I established the order of the big three in my life. Only when it was God first, family second, and work third was I really content in my job.

Principles for Financial Responsibility

Financial responsibility for Christian families can be categorized into three distinct actions concerning the resources God has entrusted to us: giving, receiving, and spending. When we discover God's principles for these three areas and implement His principles with practical strategies, our needs will be met and our families blessed. Let's look closely at each area.

Giving

Once I heard a comedian on TV say, "I've been rich and I've been poor—and I like being rich better." For the Christian, the only reason to be rich is to have resources to carry on God's program. Does God need our wealth? No. Can God's purposes be carried out without our money? Yes! God doesn't need our possessions, but we do need to give. God doesn't care how much we give as deeply as He cares why we give. When we lovingly and obediently fulfill our role as givers—no matter what the amount—God will use what we give to minister to others, and we will receive a blessing in return.

The Scriptures clearly show us many directions for our giving:

- To God through our tithes, gifts, and offerings (Proverbs 3:9-10; 1 Corinthians 16:2)
- To the poor (Proverbs 19:17)
- To other believers in need (Romans 12:13; Galatians 6:9-10)
- To those who minister to us (Galatians 6:6; 1 Timothy 5:17-18)
- To widows (1 Timothy 5:3-16)
- To family members (1 Timothy 5:8)

On the subject of giving to God, we have already determined that everything we have is His anyway. The question of how much we should actually give back to God in tithes, gifts, and offerings is debatable among Christians. Some insist on a literal tithe (ten percent) and others claim that grace allows each individual to give as he chooses. Without entering the debate, my point is simply that Christians are clearly instructed to return to the Owner of everything a portion of that which He has given to us. In this chapter I will use ten percent to represent Christian giving, whether offered as a tithe or a freewill gift.

> *Money is nothing more than a resource, and money management is nothing more than a tool to use that resource.*
>
> –Ron Blue

Second Corinthians 9:6-15 contains three excellent principles on the topic of giving. Read the passage for yourself and note the following principles:

Principle #1: We reap what we sow. If we sow sparingly, we will reap sparingly. Plants cannot grow if no seeds have been planted. Cups cannot overflow unless water is continually poured into them. If you want an abundance, you must give an abundance. If you give little, you will reap little.

Principle #2: We are to be cheerful givers. We are not to give because we feel pressured to give, but freely and joyfully as in all other areas of ministry. We have attended a couple of churches that have helped worshipers grasp this truth. In the Mariners Church in Newport Beach, California, no offering plates are passed. Church leaders believe that if God is working in your life, you will make the effort to place your gift in the mail slot in the wall. Another church we attended called the offering box in the foyer the "blessing box." Leaders in this church taught the principles of giving, then trusted parishioners to respond to God's Word instead of an offering plate. And whenever a special financial need arose, the elders brought it to the congregation, and the need was met.

Principle #3: We will be blessed because of our obedience. The world will know we are obedient to God by our faithfulness in giving.

You may ask, "How can I give before I receive? Don't I need to have something before I can give it?" That may be the way we think, but that's not the way God thinks. Luke 6:38 states, "Give, and it will be given to you." Only after we give are we ready to receive what God has for us.

Receiving

As giving Christians, we receive from several sources.

- From others giving to us (1 Corinthians 9:11)
- From diligent work (Genesis 3:19; 1 Thessalonians 4:11-12; 2 Thessalonians 3:10-13)
- From creative endeavors (Proverbs 31:13,24)
- From answers to prayer (Philippians 4:6; James 4:2)

Emilie and I know a couple in Newport Beach who once suffered serious financial problems because the husband was having difficulty finding a job. About ten couples from their church banded together to cover their house payments, food, insurance premiums, car expenses, and household needs while the man was out of work. The couple had always been faithful givers—this was their opportunity to receive. Like them, you may be surprised at times to see how God provides for your needs through the giving of others.

A primary way we receive is in return for our own hard work. With all the government programs for the needy today, sometimes we are tempted to look for a handout instead of a job. But Paul clearly confronted that attitude when he wrote, "He who does not work shall not eat" (2 Thessalonians 3:10 TLB). Your diligence as a worker is an avenue by which God will bless you and meet your needs.

Like the Proverbs 31 woman, couples may sometimes receive supplementary income from creative endeavors such as sewing, ironing, typing, woodworking, painting, or baking. Others may have the resources to open a home-based business such as selling and distributing cosmetics, cleaning supplies, kitchenwares, or nutrition items. Maybe you also have a God-given talent that you can parlay into extra income.

James wrote, "The reason you don't have what you want is that you don't ask God for it" (James 4:2 TLB). Because God owns everything we need, He is the ultimate source of everything we receive. We must ask Him to supply our needs, whether it's a certain salary, a refrigerator that is on sale, or a larger home. As we present our needs to Him, He may supply them through the giving of others, a temporary job or overtime, or a completely unknown source. But we must pray to Him and expect from Him because He is our source.

In Mark 10:29-30, Jesus teaches that if we leave houses, farms, and relatives for His sake, we will receive a hundred times as much as we give up. We have proved that this principle works. We have homes in Newport Beach, Laguna Beach, Santa Barbara, and Lake Arrowhead and vacation homes in Arizona, Illinois, and Massachusetts. We have boats and private jet planes. These assets didn't cost us one dime. They are at our disposal because they belong to Christian friends who give to us freely because somehow we have touched their lives along the way.

Spending

We first need to talk about *spendable income.* When you receive your paycheck, there is a very important number on it called *gross income,* the amount of money you earned before deductions. In order to figure your spendable income, you need to deduct two standard expenses from your gross income.

First, you must deduct your giving to God—ten percent, for example. During a session at one of our seminars, a man asked if giving should be figured on the gross or the net. A pastor in the group retorted, "Do you want to get blessed on the gross or the net?" Good point. If you are giving a percentage of your true earnings, you must figure your giving on gross income. When you consider your giving a standard expense which is taken off the top of your earnings, you will be more faithful than if you consider it an option.

Second, you must deduct local, state, and federal income taxes, approximately 17 percent, including Social Security. (Other deductions from gross income such as medical, dental, or life insurance premiums, credit union payments, payroll savings, retirement contributions, or annuities are figured elsewhere in your spending.) These two deductions equal approximately 27 percent. The 73 percent that remains we call *spendable income.* Your spendable income is the amount you have the most control over.

Some Christian financial advisors suggest that spendable income be allocated according to the 10-70-20 plan. According to this plan, ten percent of your spendable income should be reserved for savings and investments, including any deductions from your paycheck for these purposes.

General living expenses should be confined to 70 percent of your spendable income. This category includes all of the following:

- *Housing.* Housing consists of all expenses necessary to operate the home including mortgage or rent, property taxes, insurance, maintenance, and utilities. When budgeting utilities, be sure to average your payments over a 12-month period.

- *Food.* Include all groceries, paper goods, and non-food products normally purchased at a grocery store. Include items like bread and milk, which are often purchased in between regular shopping trips. Do not include lunches or dinners at restaurants these are included in another category. If you do not know your actual food expenses, keep a detailed spending record for 30 to 45 days.

- *Transportation.* In this category you have car payments, auto insurance, gas and oil, licenses, and maintenance. Another transportation expense is for depreciation, setting aside money to repair and/or replace your automobile. The minimum amount set aside should be enough to keep the car in decent repair and replace it every four or five years. If replacement funds are not available in the budget, the minimum amount set aside should cover maintenance costs. Annual or semiannual insurance premiums should be set aside monthly to avoid the crisis of a neglected expense. If you ride a bus or train to work, fares should be budgeted in this category.

- *Insurance.* Include health, life, and disability not categorized under housing or transportation. Also include amounts deducted from your paycheck for these items.

- *Entertainment and recreation.* Include vacations, camping trips, dining out, club dues, sporting equipment, hobby expenses, and athletic events. Don't forget Little League and booster club expenses. The only effective method to budget for entertainment and recreation is to decide on a reasonable amount for your family and stick with it.

- *Clothing.* Determine your monthly budget in this area by dividing a year's worth of expenditures by 12.

- *Medical.* Include insurance deductibles, doctor bills, eyeglasses, prescriptions, and over-the-counter medicines, orthodontia, and so forth.

- *Miscellaneous.* This category is a general catchall for items like child care expenses for working mothers, private education costs, allowances, laundry expenses, gifts, and so on.

The final 20 percent of your spendable income should be earmarked for payment of debts (loans, notes, credit cards) and emergencies. Sometimes called a buffer or margin, this amount consists of any money left over after expenses. Most couples with financial difficulty will not have any money in this account. Those who include a margin account in their budgets will find it to be a helpful fund for special projects, offerings, gifts, additional savings, or future education expenses.

For every $1,000 earned per month, your 10-70-20 figures would look like this:

Total income	$1,000
Less giving	(100)
Less taxes	(170)
Total spendable income	$ 730
10% savings and investments	(73)
70% living expenses	(511)
20% debts or buffer	(146)

Financial Freedom

The goal of financial responsibility is financial freedom. To be financially free you must meet these qualifications.

1. Your income exceeds your expenses.

2. You are able to pay your debts as they fall due.

3. You have no unpaid bills.

4. And, above all, you are *content* at your present income level.

If we intend to honor God with our giving, we must also honor Him with our responsible stewardship of the remaining nine-tenths of our income.

Use the Monthly Income and Expenses worksheet at the end of this chapter to evaluate your present spending habits. If your expenses are higher than your income, you can use the worksheet to identify areas where you can cut costs. You may want to consult a financial advisor for assistance.

Why Families Suffer Financially

Most of the experts in family financial counseling list three main faults which lead to financial tragedy:

1. *Failure to budget income and expenses.* Instead of telling their money where to go, many couples are always wondering where their money went. They don't chart their income and plan their expenses accordingly. They just spend what comes in—and then some.

Handling family finances must be disciplined by planning income and expenses. It's the difference between spending on purpose and by accident. Discipline in finances means you cannot always go out to dinner on the spur of the moment when your entertainment budget is low. Both partners need to be in on long-range budget planning and then help each other hold to the decisions made together. Having long-range financial goals will help you make short-range financial decisions.

2. *Failure to plan for emergencies.* Unanticipated financial emergencies consist of expenses that generally are not included in the monthly budget. They are expenses such as birthday, wedding, and Christmas gifts. Home, appliance, or auto repairs or replacement. Vacation expenses, insurance premiums, and education expenses. Because they are not predictable expenses, we usually don't plan for them, and they are a financial burden when they occur.

Emilie and I have a special emergency savings account to cover such items. Each month I write a check to this account, and we allow it to build up untouched. When an unexpected expense arrives, we transfer the needed amount from the emergency account into the checking account and pay the bill. This special fund has reduced a great deal of stress in our family. Emilie looks at me and says, "Bob, you're so smart!" My face lights up with a big smile because my leadership has been noticed and appreciated.

3. *Misuse of credit.* Banks and lending institutions are eager to let us use their money. Most of us have received occasional notices in the mail informing us that we have "qualified" for a $5,000 line of credit. Credit cards are available for a signature and sometimes sent to our homes without request. I hear some people say, "If the banks are dumb enough to send me their money, I'll take it." And that's just what the lending companies want—eager and irresponsible borrowers.

I follow a ritual in responding to unsolicited credit cards and offers of lines of credit. I hold

> *Have you found honey? Eat only what you need, that you not have it in excess and vomit it.*
>
> PROVERBS 25:16

them in my left hand, and then take a pair of scissors in my right hand and cut them up. I don't want their money because it is too easy to become a slave to credit. We have found that we would rather do without than be obligated to repayment.

Some Christian counselors suggest that we should live on a cash basis only—no credit whatsoever. For those who are in serious financial trouble, I agree that cutting up credit cards is the best solution. But I also believe credit cards have their proper place in a family's financial plan. They provide good records for spending, they are safer to carry than cash, and they help a family develop a good credit record.

But credit cards also have their shortcomings: very high interest rates, service charges, and late payment fees. Furthermore, credit card users tend to buy more than they can afford.

If families are to use credit cards, they must be mature in their financial management. Our family has only charged items that we can pay off when the statement arrives. We have rarely used our credit cards for installment purchases. The cost of credit card money is too great.

Gaining Financial Maturity

Our seminar ministry focuses on time management and home organization. Consequently Emilie and I are always thinking about how individuals and families can be more efficient in their use of time and money. We have found that the overall goal of financial maturity is achieved by taking many smaller thoughtful steps concerning income and expenses. Here are several of the helpful steps we have practiced:

- Consider God's Word as the final authority on your financial matters.

- Realize that God owns everything, and He gives to us as we demonstrate responsibility and trustworthiness with His resources.

- Remove all personal debts that do not fit into your budget. Apply for a bill consolidation loan if necessary.

- Develop sales resistance. Plan a budget within the limits of your financial goals, and then say no to any expenditure which does not fit within it.

- Concentrate on meeting your material needs before gratifying your wants.

- Look for the best buys by shopping around before purchasing. Consider buying good used items instead of new items by scouring the classified ads and secondhand stores.

- Give God the opportunity to provide your material needs. Make your requests known to Him in prayer, and ask others to pray with you about your needs.

- Become a do-it-yourself person. Instead of buying an item, consider borrowing or buying how-to books that will help you make the item at a lower cost.

- Look for ways to increase your income by using your creative skills and spare time.

- If you cannot use a credit card responsibly, cut it up or send it back and use cash.

- If you cannot dig yourself out of a financial hole, seek the help of others who are qualified. Many churches have staff members who can assist you in this area. Also consider professional counselors and local agencies that offer help in this area. Check with the Better Business Bureau for referrals.

- Help your children learn financial responsibility by teaching them at a young age the proper use of money.

WORKSHEET: Monthly Income and Expenses

INCOME

Gross Income (monthly)

Salary   _____

Interest   _____

Dividends   _____

Notes   _____

Rents   _____

Other   _____

  Total gross income   _____

Standard Expenses

Giving to God (10%)   _____

Income taxes   _____

  Total standard expenses   _____

Spendable Income

(gross income less standard expenses)   _____

EXPENSES

Savings and Investments (10%)

Savings   _____

Investments   _____

  Total savings and investments   _____

Living Expenses (70%)

Housing

  Mortgage/rent   _____

  Insurance   _____

  Property taxes   _____

  Electricity   _____

  Gas   _____

  Water   _____

Sanitation   ————

Telephone   ————

Maintenance   ————

Other   ————

Total housing   ————

Food   ————

Transportation

Payments   ————

Gas/oil   ————

Insurance   ————

Licenses   ————

Taxes   ————

Maintenance   ————

Other   ————

Total transportation   ————

Insurance

Life   ————

Medical   ————

Other   ————

Total insurance   ————

Entertainment and Recreation

Eating out   ————

Amusements   ————

Babysitters   ————

Vacation   ————

Total entertainment and recreation   ————

Clothing _____

Medical
    Doctors _____
    Dentists _____
    Prescriptions _____
    Other _____
      Total medical _____

Miscellaneous
    Toiletries/cosmetics _____
    Beauty/hair care _____
    Laundry/cleaning _____
    Allowances/lunches _____
    Subscriptions _____
    Gifts (including Christmas) _____
    Education _____
    Other _____
      Total miscellaneous _____

Total living expenses _____

Debts and Emergencies (20%)
    Credit card payments _____
    _____
    _____
    _____
    Loan and note payments _____
    Emergencies _____
    Other _____
      Total debts and emergencies _____

INCOME vs. EXPENSES

Total spendable income   _____

Total expenses (10-70-20)   _____

Monthly bottom line (income less expenses)   _____

If income exceeds expenses, where will you direct your surplus income?

If expenses exceed income, where will you increase income or cut expenses?

> *The rich rule over the poor, and the borrower is servant to the lender.*
>
> PROVERBS 22:7 NIV

May each of us, with God's help, be good stewards of all His riches. May God say to us as He did to the servant in Matthew 25:21: "Well done, good and faithful slave. You were faithful with a few things, I will put you in charge of many things; enter into the joy of your master."

Secrets to Romancing Your Marriage

- Exhibit the greatest courtesy to each other.
- Respond to your mate with a smile and sparkling eyes.
- Wife, show your husband that he is respected and the most important person in your life.
- Husband, show your wife publicly and privately how precious she is to you.
- Recognize your partner's talents, abilities, and accomplishments.
- Consistently verbalize praise and appreciation for your partner.
- Be a student of your mate. Learn who he or she is.
- Make a decision not to be critical of your mate.
- Be respectful of each other's opinions when you have a disagreement.

20

Secrets to Great Parenting

Train up a child in the way he should go, even
when he is old he will not depart from it.

PROVERBS 22:6

Our first three years of marriage were spent in a cozy paradise for two. Emilie and I did what we wanted when we wanted—trips to the beach, picnics in the park, spending money on ourselves. Then we decided to start having children. As Emilie's first due date approached, we excitedly thought about and planned for our coming child—her name, her bedroom, her colors, her clothes. Our conversations began to center around the pronoun *her* instead of *us*.

One morning Emilie went to the doctor for her routine examination. "Are you ready to have a baby?" he asked her after the exam. Emilie called me at school and asked me the same question. We were a little uncertain about this new adventure, but we were ready. All of our anticipation came to a head that evening as Jenny was born. She had finally arrived, the one we had so wanted and prayed for. Flashbulbs flashed, flowers and cards arrived at the hospital, phone calls were placed to close friends and relatives. After three days in the hospital, Emilie was able to bring our baby home.

When Jenny came through the door, our lifestyle changed drastically. Where we had been living for ourselves, we suddenly realized we had to include one other person in our family circle. Where we were once free to come and go as we pleased, we were forced to develop a schedule built around our little girl. A new and far-reaching identity had been added to our relationship as a couple. We were now parents.

Our most pressing question was, "How do we raise this new gift from God?" Lots of people on the sidelines were giving advice. Dr. Benjamin Spock had a good book on children's illnesses, which we used to diagnose a cold, measles, chicken pox, and fevers. But his philosophy about raising children was too liberal. And in those days there were no Christian books, tapes, radio programs, videos, or MOPs (Mothers of Preschoolers) groups available to parents. How were we to become equipped for our new role?

> *Anything parents have not learned from experience, they can now learn from their children.*

Instead of relying on outside help, we relied on the Bible—what it told us about children and how to raise them. We talked to other Christian parents whom we respected. We talked to both our mothers. And we prayed a lot. Our one practical goal was to raise godly children who learned to take on as much responsibility as they were capable of handling. We wanted to equip them to someday obey Genesis 2:24-25 by leaving our home to begin successful homes of their own. In this chapter we want to share some of the secrets we learned and practiced that helped us reach our goal.

The Discipline of Training

Our key verse for this chapter challenges us to "train up" our children. The word "train" has a special emphasis beyond mere talking or pleading with our children. Training is a commitment to the individual being trained. This kind of training persists through the victories and defeats of the process. We use Deuteronomy 6:7 as a basic guideline: "And you shall teach them [God's commandments] diligently to your sons and shall talk of them when you sit in your house and when you walk by the way and when you lie down and when you rise up." Training is a 24-hours-a-day, seven-days-a-week process. We are to use every life situation, wherever and whenever it happens, to train our children.

Here are three important principles that form a frame of reference for the important ministry of training your children:

1. *The influence of the parents far outweighs any other influence in your child's life.* Don't ever feel that you aren't important in the training of your child because you are "only" a parent instead of a teacher, pastor, or coach. The home holds the upper hand in determining how happy, secure, and stable a child will be. What happens in your home makes a greater impact on your child than any outside influence. This means your home life must be conducted with a purpose, a smile, an affirming touch, and an encouraging word.

Parental training and involvement have more influence on a child's success in school than the school, the quality of his teachers, or the amount of money spent on his education. Children achieve more readily when their parents read to them, value and transmit their cultural heritage to them, when families do things together, and when parents value their children's academic success.

We were visiting some friends in San Diego recently and, as we were finishing dinner, their four-year-old daughter Heather asked her daddy, "Daddy, what is the best thing that happened to you today?" Heather's daddy is a police officer, and he works in such a negative environment that his family realized they needed to deliberately speak positively. Heather's daddy answered the question, and then she went around the table asking each of us the same question. Emilie and I were impressed that our friends were building into their children uplifting experiences like Heather's question. As parents we are to uplift our children.

2. *Knowing the differences in your children's temperaments helps explain some of the difficulties in training them.* Some children are more

naturally lovable or easier to handle than others. How you relate to these differences greatly determines how your child will turn out. And some parents are more prone to nurturing than others. A nurturing parent will have an easier time training children than a nonnurturing parent. The best combination for parenting is a nurturing parent with an easy child; the most difficult combination is a nonnurturing parent with a difficult child. Being aware of the differences in temperament in yourself and your children will help you better understand how to train them.

3. *The relationship between a father and mother is critical in determining the success of a child's development.* Our first job as parents is to be the best husband and wife we can be. When children see a good relationship between Mom and Dad, they are well on their way to being emotionally balanced. If you want to have loving children, you must be a loving couple. If there is disharmony between the two of you, the children will sense it and develop insecurities at a young age. Healthy parents with a good marriage relationship produce healthy children with a good child-to-parent relationship.

> *To discipline a child produces wisdom, but a mother is disgraced by an undisciplined child.*
>
> PROVERBS 29:15 NLT

When they were children, Jenny and Brad would come to us quite often wanting to be assured that Emilie and I loved each other. When we gave them that assurance, they experienced real peace of mind. We are convinced that the stronger and healthier our bond is as husband and wife, the fewer problems we will have as parents.

If anyone must take the lead in this process, it must be the father. He must take full and total responsibility for his family. When he takes the initiative in conveying his love to his wife and children, the family will experience unbelievable rewards: a loving, appreciative, helping wife who will be her loveliest for him and children who are safe, secure, and able to grow to be their best. Emilie and I have never seen failed marriages when a husband steps up to the plate and takes charge in this area of discipline and training.

Love Them Unconditionally

We hear the term "unconditional love" quite often in the Christian community. It means "I love you no matter what you do." Unconditional love reflects the selfless agape love, which God has displayed toward us. Unconditional love is contrasted with conditional love that says, "I love you only if you do what pleases me." As parents we must love our children unconditionally, not based on what they do or don't do but on who they are—the children God gave us. We may not always like our children's behavior, but we can always love them.

Emilie and I remember when our children were in junior high school, and the popular hair length for Brad and style of dress for Jenny were different than what we preferred. Brad let his hair get longer and Jenny's style of dress was more casual than cute, but we decided to love them anyway. We didn't let length of hair or style of dress separate us from our children. We continued to love them through this transition period of their lives. And we are so glad we took this tack because today Brad is immaculate in his dress. He works as the chief operating officer for an upscale magazine here in Southern California, and he always looks like he stepped right out of *GQ* magazine. Jenny is a good example of how to dress with thrifty class. She is an expert at putting together attractive outfits from items purchased at bargain prices.

Only when we love our children unconditionally, can we prevent problems in their lives arising from guilt, insecurity, fear, and feelings of low self-esteem. If our love is conditional, our children will never be able to match our expectations. Insecurity, anxiety, and low self-esteem will haunt them as they grow into adulthood. But when we love them unconditionally, our children begin to feel good about themselves and grow to genuinely like themselves. With these positive attitudes, they will be more able to relax and control their fears and anxieties.

Children are always asking parents, "Do you love me?" The way you answer them will contribute greatly to their development. A child's behavior will reflect how he perceives your answer to this question. If he feels that you love him, he will usually behave properly. If he feels you don't love him, he will often try to gain your attention through negative behavior.

Children are always checking our verbal and nonverbal reactions to their antics to see if we really love them. Your teenagers will bring home startling news just to see how you handle the information. We recommend that you stay "cool" and don't hear or see everything.

> *Love is the basic need of human nature, for without it, life is disrupted emotionally, mentally, spiritually, and physically.*
>
> –KARL MENNINGER

Parents can nourish self-esteem in their children by letting them know that they are special, recognizing each child as an individual and avoiding comparisons between children. Concentrate on recognizing your child's efforts, not just his accomplishments. We found that immediate praise gave us the behavior we sought in our children. On the other hand, when their behavior was not what we wanted, we took equal time to discipline them. We found that when our children began to act up, they were telling us, "Mom and Dad, I don't feel loved." Emilie and I would treat their misbehavior as a signal that their needs for love were not being fully met.

Many of the problems with today's children—bad attitudes, disrespect for authority, emotional instability, drugs, crime—exist because our children do not feel genuinely loved, accepted, and cared for. Oh, we love them all right, but we haven't been able to transmit that love to them. That's because parents don't have a proper perspective on how to relate to their children. We must love and respect our children, even when their actions are different from what we want or expect.

You may be able to provide a loving influence for your children in your home, but what about the time your child spends under the influence and control of others—teachers, neighbors, peers, and even strangers? We prayed continually for God to bring good teachers, coaches, and friends into our children's lives. He answered those prayers by providing some wonderful role models for Jenny and Brad. Love your children unconditionally while they are with you and trust God to bring others into their lives who will love them also.

Focused Attention

Ever since our children were very young, both Emilie and I were present and involved in their activities at home, school, church, and community. During their formative years, our lives were centered on our children. When Brad played in a ball game, we were in the bleachers. When Jenny tried out for cheerleader, we were there to the end. For five straight years during their high school years, we attended every game Brad played and every event Jenny cheered for—whether home or away. Sometimes it was raining so hard we couldn't see the playing field. Sometimes the gym was so hot Emilie and I both sweated away five pounds. But whenever and wherever they were involved, we were there.

Did we always like being there? No! Did it cost us something to be there? Yes! Then why did we do it? Because we wanted to display our love for them through our focused attention on them and their interests. For us it was sports and athletics. For you it might be theater, orchestra, or art. Your focused attention through your physical presence and participation will make your child feel like he is the most important person in the world.

Another way we displayed focused attention on our children was through our "memory plate." Through the years we have kept a plate in the cupboard with the words "You are special" inscribed on it. Whenever a family member had a special occasion—birthday, good grades, promotion, award—we would honor the individual by serving his or her meal on the memory plate. And whenever one of the children had a disappointing day, such as not making the varsity baseball team, the memory plate was used as a way to lift up drooping spirits. We endeavored always to honor each other in our family, but the memory plate was a very special, focused honor.

> *In everything you do, put God first, and he will direct you and crown your efforts with success.*
>
> PROVERBS 3:6 TLB

A significant expression of focused attention on Jenny came when she approached her sixteenth birthday. Our family had agreed that Jenny would not be eligible to officially accept a date until she was 16, and that first date would be with Dad. What a great time I had planning this grand event. I wanted her to experience how a young lady should be treated on a date. I gave her a proper invitation, presented her with a corsage, opened the door for her, and seated her at the dinner table of a nice restaurant. We had a wonderful, open conversation that evening about boys and dating, which Jenny still talks about.

One of the family activities that really worked for us was our "family conference." We started out meeting for family conference at breakfast before church on Sunday mornings. When the children reached the fifth and sixth grades, we moved the meeting to Friday evenings. When their evenings began filling up with high school activities, we moved the meeting back to Sunday morning.

We used this time to key in on important topics brought up by Emilie, Jenny, Brad, or me. We knew that if the children were part of the decision-making process, they would be more likely to share the responsibility for the decision. If there were no particular topics to be discussed, we used the family conference for friendly conversation. This meeting was such a high priority for us that we blocked out the time on the calendar. We did not allow anything to interfere with this focused family time.

Yes, focused attention on your children will take lots of time. Time is one of our most precious commodities. We don't have enough time to fulfill all our obligations. We must be very selective in the kinds of activities we undertake. And chief among our investments should be time spent with our children.

I talked to a father recently who told me he quit his job because his boss insisted that he work 12 hours a day for six days a week. He said no to his boss and his job because he wanted to spend more time with his family than his job allowed. He paid a high price for his decision, but I'm sure God will honor his decision by leading him to another job with hours that are more conducive to family life.

Staying in Touch

When we were raising our children, there was practically no media exposure on child abuse or homosexuality. Today we are so bombarded with the reality of these problems that many moms and dads shy away from physical contact with their children, fearing they will encourage sexual disorientation. Yet research shows that children who are lovingly touched and hugged by their parents experience normal sexual development. As a classroom teacher, I found that I got along great with my students when I transmitted my acceptance to them through a hug, an arm around the shoulder, or a pat on the head. Coaches use this technique with great success in their athletic programs. Parents who love their children with physical contact are excellent role models for healthy boys and girls.

Emilie and I found that our style of physical contact varied as each child grew older. For example, when Brad was in junior high school, he announced to us that he didn't want us to kiss him in front of his friends anymore. We honored his request, but we would sneak into his room at night and kiss him while he slept.

The father plays a large part in developing proper sexual identification in his children when he meets their emotional needs for physical contact. Girls need their fathers' help in developing their self-image and sexual identity. I remember how Jenny would reach out for my approval by asking if I thought she was cute, if her dress fit properly, or if her hair looked right. The father's effectiveness in meeting his daughter's emotional needs will help her formulate these two key qualities. A father helps his daughter develop self-approval by demonstrating with his hugs that he approves of her. If a father withholds his approval and physical affection, she will find someone else—perhaps someone her parents would not approve—who will meet her need.

> *As a substitute father for hundreds of youths over the past thirteen years, I've yet to encounter a young person in trouble whose difficulty could not be traced to the lack of a strong father image in the home.*
>
> –Paul Anderson

Boys seem to call out for physical contact at an earlier age than girls. Girls don't need as much attention at the outset, but their needs increase as they approach adolescence, peaking around 11 or 12 years of age. This has significant implications for parents. I remember when Jenny, as a young lady who was already married, said, "Dad, you don't hug me as much as you used to." What an eye-opener for me! I thought she would need less physical contact from me, but she was telling me she needed more. Dad, meet your daughter's emotional needs by giving her special attention through your hugs and kisses.

Seeing Eye-to-Eye

Another important element of our parenting practice has been eye contact. Our eyes are a primary means by which we can express our love for our children. We must be careful not to love them through eye contact only when they meet our conditional standards, but to love them unconditionally with our loving looks. Dr. Ross Campbell states, "The more parents make eye contact with their children as a means of expressing their love, the more the child is nourished with love and the fuller his emotional tank."

As an elementary school teacher, I was drawn to those students who could look me in the eye when they talked to me. They were usually the most popular students in class too. When children cannot look adults in the eye, it indicates that their emotional needs are not being met. When Brad and Jenny were young, we would take their faces into our hands and ask them to look into our eyes when we wanted to talk to them. When they wouldn't look us in the eye, we knew there was some grievance of the heart or spirit. At that point Emilie and I moved into action to correct whatever was preventing their willingness to meet us eye-to-eye.

If we only use eye contact with our children in a negative way, as when we are disciplining them, the child will treat eye contact as a negative experience with parents. Some parents stare their young children down to bring about the proper behavior. But when the child gets older, he may only associate eye-to-eye contact with anger, depression, resentment, or insecurity. We must be careful to use eye contact for giving positive emotional communication.

Make Family Resolutions

There are two times of the year when we write down resolutions for the new year—New Year's Day and the beginning of the school year. Here are some suggestions:

- Don't let children watch TV or play video games on school nights (at least not until *all* their homework is completed). These activities waste a lot of creative time.

- Don't let feelings of inadequacy creep up on you because your children aren't doing well in a certain subject—or even school as a whole. The responsibility belongs to the child; however, you do need to support and encourage the learning process.

- Homework is for your children. This is the most difficult of all the resolutions. Provide an adequate study area with proper light and space. Let them know you are available to help when absolutely needed. Their responsibility is to do their homework on a timely basis. While they are studying, protect them from distractions such as loud noises, interruptions, TV, and visitors. Assist your children's schoolteachers by making sure the work is done on time.

- Don't bail your children out when they leave their lunch and books at home—or when they leave their books at school. They'll soon get the idea that it's their responsibility.

- Don't do large projects for your children. It's okay to help, but it's their responsibility to research and complete it.

- Support your child's teacher. It's so important that your child realizes that you are supporting his or her teacher. If you have a difference of opinion, set up an appointment with the teacher.

- Let your children solve their own social problems unless the situation is extraordinary. (With the increase in violence in our schools, this may not always be an easy resolution.) Children need to learn to work out their own differences.

- Teach your three Rs at home (respect, responsibility, resourcefulness) and let the teacher teach his/hers (reading, writing, and arithmetic). We need to send children to school ready to learn.

- Don't push your children into your areas of interest. Wait until they are ready and express a desire to participate. Children are often overscheduled with outside activities. It becomes a real drain on the children's energy, and it also becomes a real drain on the parent's free time.

- Let your children grow and excel in the gifts that God has given them. Most children can't be good in all subjects or be interested in all outside activities. Let them excel in their strengths.

- Let your children know that you're on their team. Show a positive interest in your children's school activities. School can do a better job of teaching your children if teachers know you are interested in your children's learning.

Talk and Talk Some More

While there are no guarantees in parenting, from my experience the most spiritually grounded children have parents who truly enjoy listening to them. The following are some ideas that foster a close relationship with me and my children and now my five grandchildren. They'll help you do the same in your family.

- *All listening doesn't need fixing.* You don't have to have a solution for everything you hear. Often children just want you to listen.

- *Look them in the eye.* When the children are young, you might have to get down on your knees. As they get older, you can stand. Eye contact is very important to being a good listener.

- *Maintain strict confidence.* You must be trusted by your children if you want them to come back again. What is said here stays here.

- *Stop what you're doing.* TV goes off, papers go down, music level is turned down. Your conversation is the number one priority for the moment.

- *No assumptions allowed.* This was hard for me because I started shaking my head no before all the facts were given to me.

- *Make sure you have warm body language.* Body language often tells more than the verbal words uttered. Be cautious about how your nonverbal language comes across. Try to keep positive as you talk.

- *Answer without minimizing the situation.* To you the item discussed might be a small deal, but to them it's a biggy. Show signs that you are really identifying with their concerns.

- *Stay in touch.* You may think your children don't want to talk, but let them know you are always interested in their lives. No matter what time of day or what topic, you are available.

- *You learn a lot through casual conversations.* Those short, 5-minute casual conversations are so valuable. Don't think that to have meaning you must visit for 30 to 60 minutes. Many times kids don't have large blocks of time. Take what you can get.

- *Make conversation part of your family tradition.* That's why having an evening meal together is so valuable. These are times when each member of the family can share feelings and ideas. Children will talk when they have the tradition of spending talking time with the family.

- *Be positive in your language.* I've found that a minimum of criticizing is best if you want frequent conversations. Talk time should be a positive experience for both parties. Negative sessions aren't fun for anyone.

- *You have ideas too.* Conversation with children isn't a one-way street. You too have opinions and should feel free to express them. You might try these questions when you think there might be a proper break in conversation: Is there anything else? Would you like to know what I think?

- *If necessary, schedule more time to talk.* Sometimes you won't be able to talk everything out. It's okay to ask, "When can we get back together to discuss this topic?" Be sure to put the date and time on your calendar.

As I view healthy families, one thing they all have in common is good communication skills. Some families are higher energy than other families. This type of family requires more talkathons than the more kick-back-and-relax families. Whatever your family style, talk and talk some more.

Secrets to Romancing Your Marriage

- ⇛ Accept your spouse's suggestions without negative body language.
- ⇛ Do what you tell your mate you are going to do.
- ⇛ Bring your husband his favorite refresher drink when he is working out in the yard on a hot summer day.
- ⇛ Remember, ladies, you're married to a sinner just like you.
- ⇛ Listen to your mate's dreams.
- ⇛ Read a book aloud to each other. Take turns reading.
- ⇛ Give her a certificate for a foot massage.
- ⇛ Give your husband time to unwind when he comes home from work.
- ⇛ After his evening bath or shower, give him a shoulder rub.
- ⇛ Bake a batch of chocolate chip cookies for your family.

21

Shaping Great Children Through Discipline

Fathers, do not provoke your children to anger, but bring them up in the discipline and instruction of the Lord.

EPHESIANS 6:4

One topic that all parents are concerned about is discipline. It seems that as a society we have not made much progress in this area. When we were new parents, Emilie and I had the same questions about discipline that abound today. All parents want good, obedient children, but we're not exactly sure how to accomplish this.

As young Christian parents, Emilie and I wanted to understand and apply scriptural principles for discipline. We relied on these verses of Scripture on the subject:

- "He who withholds his rod hates his son, but he who loves him disciplines him diligently" (Proverbs 13:24).

- "Discipline your son while there is hope, and do not desire his death" (Proverbs 19:18).

- "Train up a child in the way he should go, even when he is old he will not depart from it" (Proverbs 22:6).

- "The rod and reproof give wisdom, but a child who gets his own way brings shame to his mother" (Proverbs 29:15).

- "Fathers, do not exasperate your children, so that they will not lose heart" (Colossians 3:21).

As we endeavored to follow these guidelines, we discovered a great motivator for disciplining our children: *Rewarding good behavior is better than punishing poor behavior.* Whenever our children did something good, we would praise them, praise them, praise them. We continue this principle with our grandchildren. In our kitchen drawer we have a stack of cute bear stickers that read, "I was caught being good." When the grandchildren are over for a visit and we see one of them doing something good, we make a big deal out of it. Emilie will yell out, "I caught Bevan picking up his toys!" We apply one of the bear stickers to his T-shirt, and he is so proud. Of course the other children also want stickers, so they are encouraged to get "caught" being good. We have learned that positive reinforcement fills a child's emotional tank. And the fuller his tank, the better the child will respond to training.

As we learned to accentuate the child's positives, we also learned the value of eliminating our negatives by saying "I'm sorry" to our children when we blew it. If you don't apologize when you wrong your children, you will cause anger and resentment and short-circuit their training. Learn to apply 1 John 1:9 to these situations and then move on with the positive training of your children.

Balancing Training and Punishment

From our understanding of Scriptures, we knew that God was a God of love *and* of discipline. Emilie and I wanted to transmit love to our children through positive reinforcement before punishing them through discipline. We also knew that discipline is not only a matter of punishment, but also of training. Training is the discipline of teaching our children to do right; punishment is the discipline of correcting our children for doing wrong. One of our goals for our young children was to focus on the discipline of training. We wanted Jenny and Brad to become self-controlled, independent, and valuable members of society.

We taught values at every opportunity. We trained our children using every type of communication available. We guided them by example, provided learning experiences which were fun, provoked discussions around television programs, and devised other creative training experiences for them. We found that the better trained they were, the less punishment they needed. Our early emphasis on training led to well-disciplined children who needed a minimum of punishment. Many parents err by being too casual with training when the children are young, resulting in discipline problems as the children get older.

> *The undisciplined man is a headache to himself and a heartache to others and is unprepared to face the stern realities of life.*
>
> –AUTHOR UNKNOWN

As illustrated on the chart that follows, parents who provide strong training during the early stages of a child's growth spend less time on punishment when the child gets older. But the parent who is lax on training when the child is young will spend a lot of time and energy punishing the child as he gets older. We see misbehaving children in shopping malls, markets, churches, and schools and know that they are the products of little training in the home. We urge parents all the time, "Don't let your four-year-old control your home." At one conference on parenting we attended, a parent asked the speaker, "What do you do when your four-year-old won't put on her dress?" With little hesitation he replied, "You stuff her into it." In some cases of early training, that's what it takes.

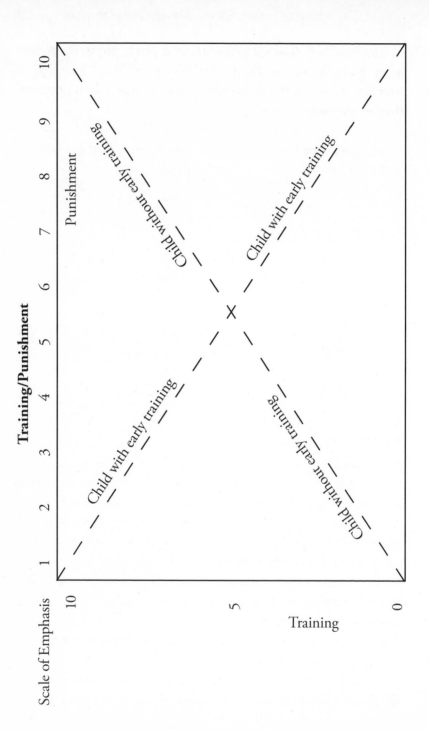

How a child responds to discipline depends primarily on how much he feels loved and accepted. As the two lists below suggest, training children with love produces a much more positive response than punishment without love.

Training with Love Produces:	Punishment Without Love Produces:
Love	Anger
Compassion	Hatred
Sensitivity	Resentment
Understanding	Defiance
Forgiveness	Resentment
Nurturing	Rebellion
Guidance	Self-centeredness
Kindness	Obstinacy
Affection	Coldness
Giving	Taking
Obedience	Resistance

The "Board of Education"

As much as we wanted to focus on the positive training of our two special, God-given blessings, there were times when we needed to apply the "board of education" through punishment. When these times came along, Emilie and I wanted to discipline them in such a way that showed them our love without provoking them to anger (see Ephesians 6:4). Through the years we developed five guidelines for the discipline of punishment. Practicing them with our children seemed to answer our concerns both for loving our children and not provoking them to anger.

First, we only punished them for defiant behavior or when a well-understood rule was broken.

Second, we reviewed with the child why he was being punished. We would ask the question, "Do you understand why you are being punished?" We continued to discuss the issue until they understood "why."

Third, from the time our children were four years old, we spanked them with a paddle on the rear end. We gave them three or four very firm swats until they cried. Over the years we had to exercise this form of punishment only a few times.

Fourth, after the swats we left their bedrooms until they stopped crying. Then we returned and again reviewed why they were punished.

Fifth, after we talked things over, we held them in our arms, hugged them, and told them we loved them. Then we ended the process with a word of prayer. We enjoy very special memories of these moments of shared love.

In this age of child abuse, some parents are reluctant to spank or punish their children for disobedience. But punishment, following God's guidelines, can be effective when administered in love. Don't punish when you are angry or emotionally out of control. Remember that the goal of punishment is to return our children to positive training.

For lesser infractions we used other forms of discipline, such as restrictions and grounding. As they reached driving age, we used the car as a pawn for discipline. The privilege of having car keys was a great motivator for positive behavior.

One Saturday afternoon, Jenny, who was a young teen at the time, was shopping with friends while Emilie and I worked in the yard. The mother of one of Jenny's friends brought Jenny home later than expected. The woman explained that the group of girls had been detained by the department store's security personnel because one of the other girls was suspected of stealing some fingernail polish.

I was so upset that Jenny was involved that, when the others had gone, I wanted to punish her immediately. But I sensed God telling me to send her to her room to read 1 John 1:9: "If we confess our sins, He is faithful and righteous to forgive us our sins and to cleanse us from all unrighteousness." I said, "Jenny, when you are ready to talk about this situation, come out and we will talk."

While she was in her room, my emotions ranged from anger to tears of disappointment. Then an amazing thing happened to me. I caught a glimpse of how God must feel about me when I sin. I realized that God has forgiven me all my unrighteousness. If God could forgive me, I could certainly forgive my daughter for being involved with a suspected shoplifter.

Jenny must have stayed in her room for at least 30 minutes, but it seemed like three hours to me. When she finally came out, she had her Bible in her hand and tears in her eyes. I gave her a big hug and told her that we loved her. We sat down together and talked and prayed about what she and the other girls had done. Together we asked God for forgiveness. I had her write the date in the margin next to 1 John 1:9. Today when she reads that verse, her mind flashes back to that Saturday when she learned that God does cleanse us from all unrighteousness when we confess our sins.

When Jenny told her friend what had happened at home, she said, "You are really lucky to have a dad like you have." Jenny felt so proud of our family, and she never had any problems like that again.

Each child responds differently to punishment. What is effective for one child may have no impact on the other children in the family. Our goal was to control our children's behavior in the most gentle and considerate way possible. After the punishment, Emilie and I always watched to see if the child was genuinely sorry for his misbehavior. We felt our punishment was effective when Jenny or Brad expressed, in words or tears, that they knew what they did was wrong, that they agreed that our standard was fair, and that they intended not to violate the standard again.

Know Your Child's Temperaments

In her book *Your Personality Tree,* Florence Littauer gives her overview of the four temperaments, so parents can better understand their children and their differences. She states, "We as parents have an obligation and duty before God to discern that way of each child and endeavor to maximize strengths and diminish weaknesses in the most loving way possible. With an understanding of temperaments, we have tools readily available."[1]

Emilie and I have found that understanding the temperaments gives parents a special grasp of the needs of each child. Far too often we parents want to change our children's temperaments to meet our expectations. But after raising our own two children and starting anew with our grandchildren, we see more clearly how important it is to discipline each child within the scope of what God wants him to be. An awareness of the four temperaments can help us do that.

The Sanguine Child

Your lively, bright-eyed sanguine child is full of curiosity and laughter. He may not always have an audience, but that never seems to stop the constant chatter that is the first step toward that center-stage personality. This child is full of wonderful, creative ideas, but is often defeated in carrying them out by a short attention span that keeps him from doing as well as others academically. Education takes a backseat to more important pursuits such as cheerleading, drama class, student council, dancing lessons, or anything else that will provide an escape from the books.

Our daughter, Jenny, is a good example of the sanguine personality. From kindergarten through high school, she was a talker in school. She was a cheerleader from the seventh grade through the first two years of college. Popularity and acceptance is an overwhelming need for this child. The sanguine child is the most likely to go along with the crowd or be drawn into an unwise situation by friends. When he tells a fib it is out of his need for approval, often gaining attention from his wild and colorful stories. Look for this child to come up with endless excuses to avoid unpleasant confrontations. A parent's disappointment or anger spells rejection for him, and he will avoid rejection at all costs. But even when the sanguine child is punished, he will soon forget the rejection and will not hold a grudge or sulk for long.

The sanguine child should be encouraged in the areas of performance—singing, dancing, acting, art, sports. Because of a short attention span, this child will have difficulty with activities such as piano, which requires diligent practice. Find at least one activity in which your child shows skill and then encourage, encourage, encourage. He will accomplish more from one word of encouragement from you than from your yelling, criticizing, or constant spanking.

This child will only do well in a duty if it is transformed into a game with a prize as motivation. Sometimes peer approval will provide the impetus, but often a parent will need to stay alongside the child until the unpleasant task is completed successfully. This child has a greater need for physical affection than those of other temperaments, so parents need to cushion their discipline with a lot of hugging, holding, and touching.

Start early to teach this child the discipline of a clean room and the importance of handling money wisely. Understand that you will need to stay right with this child to guarantee any kind of results in training. Without such a commitment from parents, this child can easily slip into irresponsibility.

The Melancholy Child

Of all the temperaments, the melancholy child is the most creative and genius-prone. Some parents actually feel threatened by the innate mental capacities of such a child. The melancholy child is deeply sensitive and has a propensity to withdraw when he really wants to reach out. In early childhood this child has a great need for physical closeness with his parents. As a result, he can be damaged by neglect or abuse during childhood more than any other personality.

These gentle, sensitive children are easily wounded and frightened. Their insecurities make them vulnerable to outside substances, offered to provide confidence or to relieve their depression. Many alcoholics, drug addicts, and homosexuals appear to be of the melancholy temperament.

The melancholy child often strives for perfection in many areas of his life. He will seldom need prodding in school, for he will be a good student with very high standards. Our son, Brad, displayed strong melancholy traits like perfectionism as early as age three. When we had catsup on the table for a meal, Brad always had to wipe off the top of the bottle before replacing the cap after use. During his three-year high school football career, Brad's team had an outstanding record of 33-3. But as a melancholy child, Brad had a difficult time with those three losses. He would dissect each play to see how his team could have won those games.

One of the great struggles for the melancholy child is in the area of negative thought patterns and a refusal to communicate his needs before his feelings are hurt. This inability to communicate causes him to internalize his need for approval rather than openly seek approval as the sanguine child will. He feels if you really love him you will sense his need for approval without him telling you. Teaching this child to communicate his needs and feelings will help to short-circuit his chronic moodiness and unhappiness.

Because he has such a vivid visual memory and tendency toward intense reaction, keep your melancholy child away from disturbing entertainment such as depressing literature and music and television programs or movies filled with horror or violence. Such input is not good for any child, but the melancholy child may be seriously affected by trauma dramas.

Beginning early in his childhood, direct the melancholy mind toward the positives of life. Spend time often having him list the good things God has done for him or given him. Teach him early that our Lord allows both successes and failures in each of our lives. Explain that each setback we face makes us more compassionate toward others who are hurting.

The Choleric Child

The choleric child is the original strong-willed child, full of energy, adventure, and impatience. This child is born to lead and expresses it early through his demands and tantrums. "Control" is the key word to understanding the choleric. Whether through his positive leadership or negative, angry outbursts, the choleric must be in control.

The choleric child can be a very productive powerhouse, able to make quick and competent decisions and often outsmarts his parents. He is full of confidence and pride and is often bossy and tactless in his relationships. When our grandson Chad was little, his choleric tendencies were evident when he pointed his finger to emphasize his statements and when he wanted his younger sister, Christine, to do things his way. When Chad was unruly, Jenny took him aside and neutralized his bossiness with a firm voice and touch.

The choleric child has the greatest potential for leadership, either positive or negative. This adventuresome child needs challenge and change. Keep him busy and give him responsibilities to help him remain productive. If he isn't in control of something, such as his room, the dog, or the backyard, he will exert his need for control on his friends at school. Because they are so bossy, cholerics often have poor peer relationships.

Because of his innate logic, he will thrive on educational toys, puzzles, and play times that allow for the expression of leadership. But since he craves control, he is always thinking and plotting way ahead of parents, teachers, and friends. As the parent of a choleric child, you must be loving and firm. He must know that you mean what you say in your training and punishment.

It is important to stand toe-to-toe with this strong-willed child in discipline no matter what the cost. You need to break his will without breaking his spirit. If you aren't consistent with your discipline and follow-through he will soon be in charge of you. Furthermore, be sure to reason sensibly with him, for he will tend to rebel when discipline or demands lack a logical explanation. Respect his need for fairness and justice and be open and honest with him, or he will catch you in your inconsistencies.

Since the choleric child is short on mercy and tenderness, it is important to utilize each of his struggles to teach him how to handle his hurts and disappointments and understand the struggles of others. Don't let him develop an attitude of superiority, which causes him to look down on others as "dummies."

The Phlegmatic Child

The easy-going phlegmatic child, who is content with a life of eating and sleeping, is seldom a problem. He requires minimal care and attention. Phlegmatics can entertain themselves easily, and it takes little to make them happy. Of all infants, they are the most calm, agreeable, and understanding. The phlegmatic child prefers to watch the world go by because watching requires less effort than getting involved. Every action is subconsciously evaluated in terms of how much energy is required, and few activities are worth the effort to him. (At times we might think that all teenagers are phlegmatics. We did.)

This child is not openly rebellious, but possesses a quiet will of iron. He may outwardly smile and agree to whatever you ask when he has no intention of complying. He may even lie to avoid any form of conflict or contention. He doesn't set out to be dishonest, but if shifting blame will eliminate responsibility, he's willing to take the chance.

While the phlegmatic child is a good listener and peacemaker, his indecisiveness and lack of motivation can paralyze him with procrastination and inactivity. A choleric parent cannot understand why a phlegmatic child has no ambition.

Emilie and Brad both masked being phlegmatics when they were young. Emilie had a very domineering father, and she didn't want to make waves, so she became a very quiet phlegmatic-like peacemaker. After we were married, she became confident in our relationship and learned to trust me. Then her true temperaments emerged—choleric and sanguine. Brad was the youngest in a very active family of sanguines and cholerics. He said, "No way am I going to tackle this group," so he masked his true temperament with passive, phlegmatic behavior. Not until he entered college and became involved in a fraternity did his natural melancholy and choleric traits fully emerge.

Because the phlegmatic is driven by his need for peace, he can become physically ill when faced with conflict. When forced to deal with another's anger, he may draw a mental blank. As such, he has a deep need to feel special to someone so don't ignore him just because he is not demanding. Value your phlegmatic child and let him know that you do.

Seek to involve this child in physical activities such as sports, gymnastics, or dancing. He may not do well in team sports because he has little drive and he may upset his teammates when he is dreaming in left field.

The phlegmatic child has the least natural imagination of all the temperaments. Begin reading to him early and stimulate his creativity through games of make-believe and mental challenge. This is the most difficult child to direct toward a lifetime work because there is little a phlegmatic gets sufficiently excited about to make him persist to a positive conclusion. Present simple choices to him and praise him warmly for making his own decisions, even if they aren't the choices you'd make.

> *If mothers would understand that much of their importance lies in building up the father image for the child, the children would turn out well.*
>
> —Samuel S. Leibowitz

This child is the most underdeveloped in the area of expressing anger. But because anger must find some form of expression, it often bubbles up in the phlegmatic as sarcasm. Help him understand the link between sarcasm and anger and how this type of humor can destroy friendships. Direct him to some creative outlets for his repressed anger through "talking out" his responses to conflict in a nonthreatening environment.

The Secret Strength of Language

Mark Twain's statement is true for adults and for kids: "I can live for two months on a good compliment." Well-chosen words will communicate your belief in your children. Your children will usually *become* what you tell them they *are*. Your words of belief in them communicate your trust, and your children will be motivated to prove themselves worthy of your trust. Galatians 6:9 states, "In due time we shall reap if we do not grow weary." There may be days when you feel like quitting because you don't see the fruit of your labor. But continue to pray and hang in there, and you will reap what you sow in your children's lives.

Secrets to Romancing Your Marriage

⋙ Buy some new lingerie for tonight—or that weekend getaway!

⋙ When you greet your spouse, give a big hug and kiss.

⋙ Eat dinner by candlelight tonight.

⋙ Tell your husband he is your superman, shining knight on a white horse, or Mr. Wonderful.

⋙ As you leave for work tomorrow, tell her you can't wait until you get home tonight.

⋙ Tell him you just love having him sleep in the same bed as you do.

22

The Law of Pursuit

Now the man [Adam] had relations with his wife
Eve, and she conceived and gave birth to Cain.

GENESIS 4:1

Have you ever thought that if your father had not pursued your mother on a cold winter night during a snowstorm, you would not be here? In Genesis 1:28, the Bible says, "God blessed them [Adam and Eve]; and God said to them, 'Be fruitful and multiply, and fill the earth.'" From the very beginning, God had a plan, and that was for man to pursue a woman and they were to be fruitful and to multiply.

In our culture the man is to be the pursuer, and the woman is to be the responder. We have reversed that process. Today the woman pursues and hopes the man will respond. But in a healthy courtship and marriage, we need to understand this law of pursuit. It is normal and very healthy for men to have an eye out for that woman of God.

Jeremiah 29:11 states, "'For I know the plans that I have for you,' declares the LORD, 'plans for welfare and not for calamity to give you a future and a hope.'" Yes, God has a plan not only for you as a husband and a wife but for your marriage too. He knows the beginning from the end. He knew you before you were in your mother's womb (Psalm 139:13-14).

How do we live out this law of pursuit? There are several things that can be done to keep your hormones flowing, your heart beating, your love growing. Here are some ideas.

Date Night

It's no mistake that this chapter follows the chapters on raising children. During your years of parenting, you must keep your marriage strong and invest in it daily. As we've mentioned earlier, once the kids are grown and gone, you are still with your spouse. If you haven't invested in one another as friends, lovers, and partners, your relationship will struggle, if not crumble.

It's a must that you both set time aside for just the two of you—no children, no friends, no relatives. A time where you can see eye-to-eye. No hiding from your mate because someone else is there to cushion the hard questions. This is a time when you both can be transparent, discuss the hard issues of life, and show respect by the way you respond to each other. You don't have to hold to the same routine each time. Change the location and the event. One time it could be dinner, another time the theater, another a romantic movie, another an action movie. Sometimes you might want to take a walk on the beach, attend a sporting event, or walk through the forest during the fall and hear the leaves crunch as you walk.

This special date tells your mate that he or she rates top priority, that you value this time and just want to be with him or her. Share a bag of popcorn or an ice cream cone. Feed the ducks at the lake. How about walking in the rain, throwing snowballs at each other (of course no rocks inside), sledding down a snow-covered slope? It doesn't have to cost much. In fact many of the most memorable times cost nothing.

To really put romance in your date, call your spouse sometime during the day and say how much you are looking forward to spending a few hours with them. Date nights work best when there is no agenda or high expectations. Just the two of you—holding hands, touching, and putting your arms around each other is a plus.

Love Basket

This idea has been a winner for so many couples over the years. In fact Emilie once received a note from a wife who made a "love basket" for her husband—the note held a picture of a newborn baby. Now that's a good result!

A love basket can be used for those very special times when you want to say "I love you" in a different way. It can be filled with food for dinner at the beach, by a lake, next to a stream. It can be taken to a ball game, a concert, or to the park. It can even be taken in your car on a love trip. It may be a surprise lunch or dinner in the backyard, in your bedroom, or under a tree. Be creative and use it to say "I love you."

Here are the things you'll need to make a love basket. First of all, you'll need a basket with a handle, preferably a heavy-duty basket, something like a picnic basket without a lid. Then you'll need a tablecloth. It can be made from a piece of fabric or from a sheet. I generally cut the tablecloth into a 45-inch square. You'll want to line the inside of your basket with this tablecloth, letting it drape over the sides, so it looks really cute. I make these for wedding shower, anniversary, or bridal gifts.

> *May the Lord bring you into an ever deeper understanding of the love of God and of the patience that comes from Christ.*
>
> 2 THESSALONIANS 3:5 TLB

Inside your basket put two fancy stemmed glasses. It's nice to use glasses with tall stems because they look pretty in the basket. You'll also need four napkins. I like to use ones with a small print, or maybe a gingham, to make the basket look fun and different. One napkin will be for the lap and the other will be used as a napkin. Fluff up your napkins and place one inside each of the glasses, so they puff up and look like powder puffs.

Next you'll need to add a nice tall candleholder and a candle. I like to use something tall because it shows over the top of the basket.

> *Let no unwholesome word proceed from your mouth, but only such a word as is good for edification according to the need of the moment, so that it will give grace to those who hear.*
>
> EPHESIANS 4:29

You'll also need a bottle of sparkling apple cider. This is non-alcoholic, but it bubbles up very nicely. (You can buy this in the juice department of your market.) You'll want a loaf of French bread. Some fresh pretty flowers will make the basket look really fun and inviting. Add some cheese, salami, dill pickles, and any other tasty treats you really like.

Love baskets are not just for the wife to give to the husband. The husband can also give one to the wife. After all, women love to be surprised by their husbands. How about kidnapping her for the weekend and journeying to your favorite place? It might be to the beach, to the mountains, to a nearby bed and breakfast. During your outing, schedule a massage, a facial, or a manicure.

Language of Love

Be sensitive with the words you use to communicate your love for each other. There are some words that encourage and build up, and there are others that are negative and tear down. A wise person will only use the plus words—those that build their mate up.

Remember you are your mate's mirror. Whenever they pass by you, they see a reflection of what you think their worth is. When you are reflecting positive reflections, they will reflect back to you positive attitudes. If you are negative, they will think negatively about themselves. Do you want to live with someone who is positive or one who is negative? Pay attention to the words you speak most often. Use language that reflects your love for your spouse.

Positive Words	Negative Words
I love you.	I don't love you.
This is a good meal.	You always mess up a good recipe.
You are a good mom.	The children are off the chart.
I appreciate how you take care of our home.	Things are a mess.
I love the candlelight.	The candles will set the house on fire.
What a pretty new dress.	You look fat in that dress.
I love your new hair style.	You new haircut makes you look ten years older.
I love how you take time to make our dining room table look so inviting.	Why waste all your time decorating the dining table?
The music you have playing is so relaxing.	Turn off that soft stuff. Let's hear some music with action.

It all depends on how you set the stage—words play such an important part in determining if you're using the proper love language. Your spouse will respond positively or negatively, depending on the words you use. Don't expect to get a positive response, if you use negative words. You can't expect tonight to be the night if you are tearing down your mate. Your intimacy will be no greater than the language of love you speak.

Just Think About It

As a couple gets older and schedules get crowded, you have to plan for intimacy. We have come up with a way to "telegraph" our desires to one another. We've placed a colorful card in our bathroom drawer that reads: *Just think about it.*

Either one of us has the freedom to pull this card out of the drawer and display it for the other to see. The card is a signal that one partner has been having romantic thoughts and would like to plan a romantic evening in the near future.

Although the man will usually display this sign most often, the woman doesn't always wait for him. It's okay for the wife to show romantic desires for her husband. Don't be bashful. Remember, after each creation God said that it was good. He meant for His people to enjoy their sexuality. God instituted the law of pursuit. It's good!

Give a Daily Hug

Touching plays such a healthy role in telling another person you love them. There is something that is very positive when your mate holds your hand, puts their arms around you, gives you a pinch, gives you a peck on the cheek, and blows a breath on your neck. We try to make a daily habit of giving at least one hug every day. Each morning before I put my socks and shoes on, Bob rubs my legs and feet with a soothing lotion. It's just another way he says that he loves me.

Share Your Heart

Life is so exciting when each of you brings your dreams to the table. Get to the point in your marriage where you are able to be transparent in your conversation. Your dreams don't always have to be accomplished tomorrow. Some of our best dreams are planned for five to ten years in the future. Dreams are what you live for. Fulfillment of one's dreams is what makes the two of you become one. In Genesis 2:25, we read that Adam and Eve were naked and not ashamed of it. This is a beautiful picture of two people being transparent about their dreams and hopes. Couples respond when they can trust that their mates are truly interested in their innermost thoughts. Dare to dream together. Don't look back over life and end up sorry because you didn't include your spouse in your thought process. Risk your egos and share heart-to-heart conversations. Ask questions like:

- If you could talk to God face-to-face and ask Him one question, what would it be?
- What is your happiest memory?
- What would be your ideal vacation?
- If you only had one day left to live, how would you spend it?
- If you could start over at a specific time in your life, when would that be?
- What is your deepest fear?

Yes, there is a law of pursuit, and I challenge you to never stop pursuing your spouse. Be creative in how you keep the flame alive. Don't let it die down. Use the secrets we've shared in this book and the secrets you discover during your marriage journey to rekindle the flame and make your marriage a spark of light in the world.

Secrets to Romancing Your Marriage

- Remember, happily married people do exist.
- Don't be afraid to flirt with each other.
- Remember to listen more than you talk.
- Be your mate's best cheerleader.
- Love so that your marriage gets stronger and better over the years.
- Remember that you were husband and wife before you were parents.
- Sexual satisfaction is part of God's design for marriage.

⇛ It's okay to kiss when you are stuck in traffic.

⇛ It's okay to give your mate a compliment when out in public.

⇛ Look and believe in your spouse's full potential

⇛ Spend time uncovering the secrets that make your marriage thrive.

⇛ Spend time sharing what you've learned with other couples and with your kids.

Notes

Chapter 1—I Pledge You My Troth

1. Elon Foster, ed., *6000 Sermon Illustrations* (Grand Rapids, MI: Baker Book House, 1992), p. 639.

Chapter 2—Looking for Love

1. Helen Keller, *The Story of My Life* (Whitefish, MT: Kessinger Publishing, LLC, 2003), pp. 29-31.

Chapter 6—After the Wedding

1. Larry Crabb, *The Marriage Builder* (Grand Rapids, MI: Zondervan, 1982), p. 122.
2. Denis Waitley, *Seeds of Greatness Treasury* (New York, NY: Pocket Books, a division of Simon Schuster Inc., 1983), p. 160.

Chapter 7—Simple Secrets Every Wife Should Know

1. Dennis and Barbara Rainey, *Building Your Mate's Self-Esteem* (San Bernadino, CA: Here's Life Publishers, 1986), p. 35.

Chapter 8—Simple Secrets Every Husband Should Know

1. Dennis and Barbara Rainey, *Building Your Mate's Self-Esteem* (San Bernadino, CA: Here's Life Publishers, 1986), p. 56.
2. Jay Adams, *Christian Living in the Home* (Grand Rapids, MI: Baker Book House, 1972), pp. 91-92.

Chapter 11—Growing Together Despite Differences

1. Doreen Kimura, "Male Brain, Female Brain: The Hidden Differences," *Psychology Today*, November 1985, p. 56.
2. William and Nancy Carmichael with Dr. Timothy Boyd, *That Man! Understanding the Difference Between You and Your Husband* (Nashville, TN: Thomas Nelson, 1980), adapted from chapter 2.
3. Dr. Daniel G. Amen, M.D., *Healing the Hardware of the Soul* (New York: The Free Press, 2002), p. 66.
4. Adapted from Warren Farrell, *Why Men Are the Way They Are* (New York: McGraw-Hill, 1986), p. 139.
5. Carol Gilligan, *In a Different World* (Cambridge, MA: Howard University Press, 1981), p. 8.

6. Mary Conroy, "Sexism in Our Schools: Training Girls for Failure," *Better Homes and Gardens,* February 1988, pp. 44-48.

Chapter 12—Meeting Your Wife's Needs

1. Willard F. Harley, Jr., *His Needs, Her Needs* (Grand Rapids, MI: Revell, 1986), p. 19.
2. Dr. Kevin Leman, *Sex Begins in the Kitchen* (Grand Rapids, MI: Revell, 1999).

Chapter 13—Meeting Your Husband's Needs

1. Dr. Toni Grant, *Being a Woman* (New York: Random House, 1988), p. 46.
2. Willard F. Harley, Jr., *His Needs, Her Needs* (Grand Rapids, MI: Revell, 1986), p. 10.
3. Ibid., p. 78.
4. Ibid., pp. 130-35.

Chapter 14—Four Marriage Health Builders

1. David Augsburger, *Sustaining Love* (Ventura, CA: Regal Books, 1988).

Chapter 15—Keep Listening and Talking

1. Dwight Small, *After You've Said I Do* (Westwood, NJ: Fleming H. Revell, 1968), p. 244.
2. H. Norman Wright, *Communication: Key to Your Marriage* (Ventura, CA: Regal Books, 1974), p. 52.
3. John Powell, *Why Am I Afraid to Tell You Who I Am?* (Niles, IL: Argus Communications, 1969), adapted from pp. 54-62.
4. Florence Littauer, *After Every Wedding Comes a Marriage* (Eugene, OR: Harvest House, 1981), adapted from pp. 168-76.
5. H. Norman Wright, *Communication: Key to Your Marriage* (Ventura, CA: Regal Books, 1974), adapted from pp. 71-77.

Chapter 18—Making Your Wife Your Best Friend

1. Bob Barnes, *500 Handy Hints for Husbands* (Eugene, OR: Harvest House Publishers, 2006), pp. 255-59.

Chapter 21—Shaping Great Children Through Discipline

1. Florence Littauer, *Your Personality Tree* (Nashville, TN: Thomas Nelson, 1989), pp. 160-70.

Harvest House Books by Bob & Emilie Barnes

Bob & Emilie Barnes

*15-Minute Devotions
for Couples*

Be My Refuge, Lord

*A Little Book of Manners
for Boys*

*Minute Meditations
for Couples*

Bob Barnes

5-Minute Bible Workouts for Men

*15 Minutes Alone
with God for Men*

Men Under Construction

*What Makes a Man
Feel Loved*

Emilie Barnes

The 15-Minute Organizer

15 Minutes Alone with God

*15 Minutes of Peace
with God*

*15 Minutes with God
for Grandma*

101 Ways to Clean Out the Clutter

*500 Time-Saving Hints
for Every Woman*

Christmas Teas of Comfort and Joy

Cleaning Up the Clutter

*Emilie's Creative
Home Organizer*

*Everything I Know
I Learned in My Garden*

*Everything I Know
I Learned over Tea*

Friendship Teas to Go

Garden Moment Getaways

Good Manners for Every Occasion

A Grandma Is a Gift from God

Heal My Heart, Lord

Home Warming

If Teacups Could Talk

I Need Your Strength, Lord

An Invitation to Tea

Journey through Cancer

Let's Have a Tea Party!

A Little Book of Manners

A Little Hero in the Making

A Little Princess in the Making

The Little Teacup that Talked

Meet Me Where I Am, Lord

Minute Meditations for Busy Moms

*Minute Meditations for Healing
and Hope*

More Faith in My Day

More Hours in My Day

The Quick-Fix Home Organizer

A Quiet Refuge

Safe in the Father's Hands

*Simple Secrets to
a Beautiful Home*

A Tea to Comfort Your Soul

*The Twelve Teas®
of Friendship*

The Twelve Teas® of Inspiration

Walk with Me Today, Lord

What Makes a Woman Feel Loved

Youniquely Woman